Promoting Resilience in the Classroom

The 'Innovative Learning for All' series
Series editor: Professor Paul Cooper

The 'Innovative Learning for All' series features accessible books that reveal how schools and educators can meet the needs of vulnerable students, encouraging them to engage in learning and to feel confident in the classroom. Grounded in the latest innovative practice and research, these books offer positive guidance on improving the educational standards for all children by ensuring the most vulnerable are supported.

also in the series

Nurture Groups in School and at Home
Connecting with Children with Social, Emotional and Behavioural Difficulties
Paul Cooper and Yonca Tiknaz
ISBN 978 1 84310 528 2

of related interest

The Bullies
Understanding Bullies and Bullying
Dennis Lines
ISBN 978 1 84310 578 7

Understanding School Refusal
A Handbook for Professionals in Education, Health and Social Care
M. S. Thambirajah, Karen J. Grandison and Louise De-Hayes
ISBN 978 1 84310 567 1

Helping Children to Build Self-Esteem
A Photocopiable Activities Book
2nd edition
Deborah M. Plummer
Illustrated by Alice Harper
ISBN 978 1 84310 488 9

Helping Adolescents and Adults to Build Self-Esteem
A Photocopiable Resource Book
Deborah M. Plummer
ISBN 978 1 84310 185 7

Anger Management Games for Children
Deborah M. Plummer
Illustrated by Jane Serrurier
ISBN 978 1 84310 628 9

Self-Esteem Games for Children
Deborah M. Plummer
Illustrated by Jane Serrurier
ISBN 978 1 84310 424 7

Promoting Resilience in the Classroom

A Guide to Developing Pupils'
Emotional and Cognitive Skills

Carmel Cefai

Foreword by Paul Cooper

Jessica Kingsley Publishers
London and Philadelphia

The author and publishers are grateful to the proprietors listed below for permission to quote the following material: Figure 4.2 from *Building School Communities* (1994) by T. Sergiovanni. San Francisco, CA: Jossey-Bass. Reproduced with permission from John Wiley & Sons, Inc. Figure 6.2 from *Responding to Student Diversity: Teacher's Handbook* (2007) by P. Bartolo, I. Janik, V. Janikova, T. Hofsass et al. Malta: University of Malta. Reproduced with permission. Figure 9.4 from 'Managing Complex Change Toward Inclusive Schooling' by J. S. Thousand and R. A. Villa, in *Creating an Inclusive Classroom* by R. A. Villa and J. S. Thousand (eds) (1995). Alexandria, VA: Association for Supervision and Curriculum Development. Reproduced with permission.
We have made every reasonable effort to trace all copyright-holders of quoted material, apologise for any omissions and are happy to receive emendations from copyright-holders.

First published in 2008
by Jessica Kingsley Publishers
116 Pentonville Road
London N1 9JB, UK
and
400 Market Street, Suite 400
Philadelphia, PA 19106, USA

www.jkp.com

Library of Congress Cataloging in Publication Data
Cefai, Carmel.
Promoting resilience in the classroom : a guide to developing pupils' emotional and cognitive skills / Carmel Cefai ; foreword by Paul Cooper.
p. cm.
Includes bibliographical references and index.
ISBN 978-1-84310-565-7 (pb : alk. paper) 1. Classroom management. 2. Resilience (Personality trait) in children. I. Title.
LB3013.C368 2008
370.15'3—dc22
2007044971

British Library Cataloguing in Publication Data
A CIP catalogue record for this book is available from the British Library

ISBN 978 1 84310 565 7

Printed and bound in Great Britain by
Athenaeum Press, Gateshead, Tyne and Wear

This book is dedicated to the primary and
secondary school teachers who instilled in me
a never-ending love for learning.

Acknowledgements

The author would like to thank Paul Cooper, Series Editor, not only for inviting me to write this book, but for his continuous encouragement, support and advice. His guidance and feedback, and his extensive experience and knowledge in this area, have been invaluable during the writing of the book. Thanks are also due to Stephen Jones, Karin Knudsen and Lucy Mitchell at Jessica Kingsley Publishers for their patience and support and for ensuring that this book was completed on time. This book would not have been possible without the contributions of the heads of school, classroom teachers and pupils who participated in the study on which this book is based. I am greatly indebted for their time and their generosity and for sharing their experiences, their thoughts and their feelings with me. Thanks also to Chris Watkins, supervisor of the PhD on which this book is largely based, for his continuous guidance and support. Finally a word of thanks goes to David Pisani who helped in the design of the diagrams and tables in this book, and to my brother Joe for the initial proofreading.

Carmel Cefai

Contents

Part 3: A Plan of Action for the Classroom Practitioner

List of Figures

List of Case Studies

List of Tables

List of Boxes

Series Editor's Foreword

The twin needs to raise educational standards for all and to improve access to educational opportunities for the most vulnerable members of society continue to be major challenges facing educators throughout the world. The persistent link between socio-economic status and educational attainment is one of the few truly dependable outcomes of social scientific research. Children who come from socially deprived backgrounds are at much greater risk of educational failure than children who come from more privileged backgrounds. In the USA, in 1979 individuals from the top income quartile were four times more likely to successfully complete a four-year college degree programme than individuals from the bottom quartile (Barton 1997). By 1994 the disparity had increased from 4 to 10 times (*ibid.*). In the UK similar concerns have been noted by the DfES (2004). There is a further association between educational failure and social, emotional and behavioural difficulties (*ibid.*), as well as an association between social, emotional and behavioural problems and social disadvantage (Schneiders, Drukker, Ende *et al.* 2003).

The interaction between socio-economic, educational and socio-emotional factors is clearly complex and multi-faceted. It is certainly not the case that any one of these factors necessarily precedes either of the others. Resilience factors of various kinds come into play for some people, enabling them, as individuals, to buck the statistical trends. Temperament, social and cognitive strategies, personal values, external social support structures, and parental personality characteristics, can help to create opportunities for unpredicted positive educational and socio-emotional outcomes for individuals who appear to be in the most dire socio-economic circumstances (Rutter 1987). Unfortunately, there are counter-balancing risk factors, which will combine with disadvantage for other people to create serious life problems (e.g. Patterson, Reid and Dishion 1992).

It is all too easy to place the blame for a child's educational failure and disruptive behaviour on family and/or neighbourhood factors, and to write off whole geographical areas as being populated by 'undesirables'. It is perhaps because of the dangers of provocative, negative stereotyping of this kind that we sometimes neglect the socio-economic correlates of educational disengagement and social, emotional and behavioural difficulties.

11

A crucial factor that can be both a cause and effect of educational failure is what David Smith, in the Edinburgh Study of Youth Transitions and Crime, describes as 'attachment to school' (Smith 2006). Attachment to school can be defined in terms of the degree of commitment towards and engagement with schooling that students feel. Students who have a strong attachment to school have feelings of attachment to teachers, and believe that success in school will lead to significant rewards in later life. Weak attachment to school is characterised by indifference or hostility towards teachers and scepticism about the value of schooling. Weak attachment to school can lead to disaffection and alienation. These are problems of a psychological nature that impair the individual's capacity for social and academic engagement that can, in turn, lead to reduced life chances.

Innovative Learning for All offers a series of publications each of which considers ways in which schools in the 21st century can address the needs of vulnerable students and contribute to their effective attachment to school and engagement with educational opportunities. Each author in the series offers insights into different ways in which these goals can be achieved by drawing on the best available, and in some cases original, research evidence. At the heart of the series is the shared view that educational standards for everyone will improve if we focus our efforts on promoting the educational engagement of the most vulnerable. There is also a strong consensus around the need to value all children and young people as individuals and to maintain a commitment to their positive growth, and for these values to be translated into practical support that is informed by a firm conceptual and technical understanding.

This is not to say that education is a cure-all for the dysfunctions of society. Far from it, the ideas and practices described in this series depend upon political will and government action to achieve their best. On the other hand, the programmes and approaches dealt with in this series will not be made redundant by enlightened and effective measures that address social and economic deprivation. However, they will, undoubtedly, be aided by such measures. It follows, therefore, that the authors in this series all hope that some of the ideas that they put forward will contribute to both the thinking and practice of educators as well as of politicians.

Paul Cooper, University of Leicester

REFERENCES

Barton, P.E. (1997) *Towards Inequality: Disturbing Trends in Higher Education.* (Report number: PIC-INEQUALITY). Princeton, NJ: Educational Testing Service.

DfES (2004) *Breaking the Cycle.* London: DfES.

Patterson, G., Reid, J. and Dishion, T. (1992) *Anti-Social Boys*, Vol. 4. Eugene, OR: Castalia.

Rutter, M. (1987) 'Psychosocial resilience and protective mechanisms.' *American Journal of Orthopsychiatry 57*, 3.

Schneiders, J., Drukker, M., van der Ende, J., Verhulst, J., van Os, J. and Nicolson, N. (2003) 'Neighbourhood socio-economic disadvantage and behavioural problems from late childhood into early adolescence.' *Journal of Epidemiology and Community Health 57*, 699-703.

Smith, D. (2006) *School Experience and Delinquency at Ages 13 to 16.* Edinburgh: Centre for Law and Society, University of Edinburgh.

CHAPTER 1

Educational Resilience for All

In the centre of the Mediterranean Sea lies a small island with crystal blue water, gentle flat-topped hills, green fertile valleys and small ancient villages basking in the warm sunshine. Its rich historical heritage is epitomised in the Ggantija Neolithic Temples, the oldest free-standing structure in the world, predating the Egyptian Pyramids by a thousand years. Gozo is part of the Maltese archipelago, situated at the crossroad of the Mediterranean between Europe and North Africa. The Gozitans are a friendly and hardworking people. One of their most marked characteristics is their resilience. Theirs is a story of survival in the face of abandonment, of growth and prosperity in the face of exploitation, poverty and marginalisation. In 1551 the island was ravaged by Ottoman corsairs and the whole population was taken into slavery in North Africa. In times of invasion, it was abandoned by the military authorities. As late as the Second World War Gozo was considered militarily unimportant and would have been the first to be occupied by the Axis forces had the planned invasion taken place. Yet it was the Gozitan farmers who saved the Maltese islands from capitulation by providing badly needed flour until supplies arrived on the warships. Despite its limited resources, the island has managed to thrive by exploiting its strengths, namely the fertility and natural beauty of the land, the hard work and resourcefulness of its people, and the strong sense of community and connectedness among the inhabitants.

The Gozitan experience is one of a people thriving against a background of hardship and poverty. It is one of resilience; that is, the ability to overcome the odds and succeed in the face of adversity. Resilience draws our attention to growth in the presence of risk, to what helps us succeed rather than what keeps us back. By studying the success story of individuals, families and communities, we are then able to promote those qualities and systems which facilitate the success of individuals who are at risk in one way or another. In education this has been translated into initiatives to create social systems which protect children and young people coming from adverse social-economic backgrounds, and which facilitate their healthy cognitive and socio-emotional development and, consequently, their 'graduation' as successful young adults prepared for the tests of life.

PREPARING CHILDREN AND YOUNG PEOPLE FOR THE TESTS OF LIFE

As they seek to establish themselves as autonomous and successful citizens in a fast-changing world, young people, whether at risk or not, will need to have the required competencies and resources to achieve their goals, to solve problems effectively, to engage in healthy relationships and to sustain their psychological and social wellbeing. When they leave school, they will have to have learned the requisite academic skills to enable them to function as self-reliant citizens and to gain access to opportunities and resources. They will also need to be equipped with other skills: to be flexible in the face of change; to be creative in problem solving and effective in decision making; to build and maintain supportive relationships; to work collaboratively with others; and to mobilise their resources in times of difficulty. They will have to be able to steer clear of crime, violence, substance abuse, unwanted teenage pregnancy, poverty and social exclusion, as well as being resilient, both academically and socio-emotionally, in the face of an unstable, changing society. Academic and socio-emotional literacy, however, are not mutually exclusive or developed at the expense of one another. Indeed, they can support, reinforce and complement each other. Happy and socially competent individuals are in the end more productive in schools and society (Layard 2005). This dual focus in education is both desirable and essential in today's world, and also possible to achieve. This book is about this broader vision of education. It is about the formation of academically and socially resilient students prepared for the tests of life rather than a life of tests (Elias 2001). It is rooted in a psycho-educational perspective which underlines a positive and proactive view of human development and behaviour. It proposes a model of classrooms operating as protective contexts for children's and young people's development. Within this universal model of educational resilience, classrooms operate as optimum learning environments for all their pupils, including those considered at risk, promoting their cognitive, social and emotional competence.

The book provides a framework which can be modified and applied by schools and classrooms according to their needs, and which includes classroom practitioners, in collaboration with staff, pupils and parents, in designing, implementing and evaluating their own action plans. It has originated from a study of classroom practices, with examples generated from actual classrooms. It is intended as a practical guide for classroom practitioners and educationalists engaged in school improvement and development, in promoting educational engagement and socio-emotional competence in the classroom. Besides classroom teachers, the book should appeal to heads of school, support and specialist teachers, learning support assistants, school counsellors and educational psychologists. Teacher trainers and INSET providers may find the theoretical framework and the action plan very accessible and easy to use in their teacher education courses. The book could also serve as a resource for educationalists engaged in policy making, planning and curriculum development, with particular reference to social and emotional learning.

OUTLINE OF THE BOOK

The book is divided into three major parts. The first part proposes a theoretical model of classrooms as resilience-enhancing contexts for all the pupils. The definition of educational resilience proposed in the second chapter diverges from traditional ones in that it is not based exclusively on risk. It suggests a universal approach focused on protective factors which operate for both at-risk and non-at-risk pupils. This book is for the promotion of social and academic competence for all pupils, including those perceived as being at risk. Chapter 3 then presents the model that has been developed from the study of processes occurring in primary school classrooms, characterised by good practice in educational engagement and socio-emotional competence. The model describes how contextual processes and facilitating forces promote engagement and socio-emotional competence in the classroom.

The second part of the book is an elaboration of the theoretical model in relation to actual classrooms. It presents various narratives and stories from classrooms selected for their good practice in educational engagement and socio-emotional competence. The chapters in this part of the book provide a number of points where you will be invited to reflect on particular aspects of your practice. The first chapter (Caring Classrooms) presents various illustrations of how classroom teachers sought to build caring relationships with their pupils. Classroom relationships are examined further in Chapter 5 (Prosocial Classrooms), with illustrations of relationship building among the pupils themselves. The next three chapters present various facets of pupil engagement in the classroom. Chapter 6 (Engaging Classrooms) focuses on meaningful and inclusive engagement, providing examples of how various teachers created authentic, experiential and enjoyable learning experiences. Chapter 7 (Collaborative Classrooms) highlights the benefits of pupils building knowledge together and of classroom teachers collaborating with their pupils, their colleagues and the parents in their practice. The final chapter in this part

(Empowering Classrooms) focuses on influential engagement, providing examples of pupils being encouraged to make choices, participate in decisions and believe in themselves as competent learners.

Part 3 (Chapter 9) is a reflective developmental section that helps you to implement the resilience-building model in your own classroom. Classroom change is suggested through an action research framework that guides you, in partnership with the pupils, colleagues and parents, through an ongoing process starting with an assessment of the present situation, the formulation of a plan of action, the implementation of the plan, evaluation and further change.

The main aim of the book is to empower school and classroom staff to take responsibility for their own and their pupils' development, to take self-generated and self-directed action in seeking to engage the pupils in meaningful and influential learning experiences within a caring and collaborative culture.

PART 1

A MODEL FOR CLASSROOM PRACTITIONERS

CHAPTER 2

Introducing Risk and Resilience in Education

In this chapter the concept of resilience is explored within an educational context. The chapter starts by examining the paradigm shift that took place in moving from risk to resilience and how the problems with the former have led to the emergence of the latter: a model emphasising growth and strength development. Another shift in the definition of educational resilience is then proposed. Resilience is construed within a 'universal' perspective, focusing on common processes that promote positive social and academic behaviours among normally developing children and young people as well as those who may be at risk in their development. The chapter concludes with a contextual and universal definition of educational resilience.

RISK

St Mark's Primary School is situated in a relatively socially disadvantaged region in Malta. In the early 1980s the school had 350 students, the great majority coming from the low socio-economic group. The school was struggling with high rates of illiteracy, absenteeism and misbehaviour, as well as the parents' lack of cooperation and occasional abuse of staff. Teacher stress was very marked, with a high turnover of staff every year. St Mark's was considered a failing school, and the pupils attending the school were at risk of educational failure. As part of the Education Priority Areas' policy at the time, the local education authority (LEA) provided extra funding and support to the school to reduce disaffection and increase attendance and achievement. More staff were assigned to the school, including more teachers, so that classrooms could be reduced in size. An additional assistant head was appointed, together with extra support staff such as learning support teachers and classroom assistants. More regular service from educational psychologists, educational social workers, school counsellors and school doctors and nurses was made available to the school. A welfare fund was set up to address the basic needs of some of the pupils and their families, such as the provision of free uniforms, stationery, textbooks and lunches. In some cases, financial assistance was provided to the families themselves, who were also receiving assistance from the social workers. The complementary teaching room was furnished with state-of-the-art resources, and an office was opened for the support professionals visiting the school. The school environment was also enhanced with new furniture, more comfortable classrooms and improved play facilities.

The above example illustrates how earlier approaches to the educational success and failure of school children have largely been focused on the identification of risk factors with their adverse effects on development, and the introduction of measures to counteract such effects. Within such a perspective children and young people coming from socio-economically deprived backgrounds, ethnic minorities or adverse family circumstances are considered as being at risk in their development and success at school. The term 'at risk' is a broad one, with numerous factors being considered as likely to compromise children's development, such as poverty, abuse and neglect, developmental disability, and parental illness or psychopathology. In education it usually refers to children and young people who are at risk of school failure by virtue of coming from a disadvantaged background such as a deprived socio-economic background, region, ethnic status, family circumstances and language (Organisation for Economic Co-operation and Development (OECD) 1995). The main focus of such an approach has been to identify the factors that put pupils' success in school at risk and then to remedy and/or prevent such factors (cf. 'fixing kids' approach). As illustrated above, a common practice has been to provide additional funding to schools which have a preponderance of pupils coming from disadvantaged socio-economic backgrounds, such as pupils eligible for free lunch or whose parents were in receipt of unemployment benefits.

The risk model in education has come under increasing scrutiny in recent years. Children and young people have been found to develop successfully despite risk and adversity, and what may be an obstacle to development for one child may be an opportunity for another (Liddle 1994; Semmens 1999). Individual children may be considered at risk when in actual fact they are not. Expectations for entire groups of children may be suppressed, while learning and behaviour problems may be interpreted as related to individual deficits or the group's 'culture of poverty' (Catterall 1998). A risk orientation is also likely to lead to the labelling of children, families and communities because of the children's difficulties while ignoring those characteristics of the school context which may fail to promote children's cognitive and social development. Finally, the provision of extra resources to schools considered at risk has not necessarily been accompanied by marked improvements in expected outcomes. For instance, Cappella and Weinstein (2001), making use of a national, longitudinal database, found that, while 15 per cent of the at-risk group (pupils coming from disadvantaged backgrounds) improved their reading performance significantly over their secondary school years, the remaining 85 per cent either dropped out of school or remained in the lowest or basic achievement level. As Pianta and Walsh (1998, p.408) put it, 'we have not been very successful at helping poor children succeed in school...despite decades of intervention programmes, substantial success stories have been few'.

> Despite the definition and redefinition of 'at risk', one thing which has remained constant is the belief that some parents have failed their children, reflecting deep seated biases against women, the poor and ethnic groups. (Lubeck and Garrett 1990, p.327)

RESILIENCE

It was the failure of the risk model to explain success and failure at school adequately that led to a paradigm shift towards models of resilience and competence enhancement. Both the risk and resilience perspectives are concerned with understanding what helps children and young people to do well at school. However, while for the former this represents problem avoidance, the latter is concerned with wellbeing and health in addition to dysfunction (Luthar, Cicchetti and Becker 2000; Waxman, Brown and Chang 2004). It shifted the focus from deficit and disadvantage to growth and strength development. It asks 'What makes children in difficulty achieve and be successful?' rather than 'What prevents children in difficulty from succeeding?' Through the study of children and young people who managed to thrive and be successful at school despite negative circumstances in their lives, the resilience perspective has led to a reconsideration of the ways in which schools can foster success in children and young people (Brown, D'Emidio-Caston and Benard 2001; Henderson and Milstein 1996). It suggested that we may be more effective in supporting children's and young people's development and wellbeing by focusing on their strengths rather than on their weaknesses.

There are various definitions of resilience, but a common theme in most definitions is that of competence and success despite severe and prolonged adversity and disadvantage (Luthar et al. 2000). Benard (1991) describes resilience as a set of qualities or protective mechanisms that give rise to successful adaptation despite the presence of high-risk factors during the course of development. Educational resilience studies have mainly concentrated on the academic achievement of children coming from adverse environments, such as poverty, the inner city and ethnic minorities. The early studies of the 1970s construed resilience in terms of individual invulnerability, and focused on individual characteristics, such as problem-solving skills and stress resistance, which 'harden' children and young people growing up in a difficult environment and enable them to achieve success (Anthony 1974; Garmezy 1971). As later studies were to show, however, positive outcomes in the face of adverse circumstances are also influenced by other processes besides individual characteristics, including the family, the school and the community. Development is the result of the dynamic interactions between the various systems impinging on the child's life (Bronfenbrenner 1979), and it is the interaction between the child and his or her environment that finally determines the adaptive process.

> The key to developing resiliency in children is opportunities, both plentiful and meaningful. Opportunities to rest from resisting a hostile environment, opportunities to explore in safety and security, opportunities to believe and to dream. (Katz 1977, as quoted in Condly 2006, p.228)

The notion of invulnerability gradually gave way to that of resilience, and the earlier focus on individual characteristics subsequently changed to the identification of protective factors that moderated the impact of risk factors (Garmezy and Rutter 1983; Garmezy, Masten and Tellegen 1984; Werner 1990). Seminal studies such as those by Werner and Smith (1988, 1992) and Garmezy and Rutter (1983) found that, despite the high-risk environments in which their participants grew up, the majority developed into healthy, successful young adults. They reported that protective factors have a stronger impact on children's development than risk factors. Subsequent literature identified three broad sets of factors that protected vulnerable children and facilitated their development into competent and autonomous young adults. These are: the dispositional attributes of the individual (social competence, problem-solving skills, autonomy and a sense of purpose); the family, particularly in the early years; and external support systems such as the school. It is the interactions of these three protective systems in the child's life that eventually lead to success in the face of adversity (Dent and Cameron 2003; Pianta and Walsh 1998; Wang and Haertel 1995). Individuals with high levels of these personal and social protective factors are thus more effective in coping with adversity than individuals with lower levels of protection.

Resilience is a dynamic process that occurs in a context and is the result of the person in interaction with his or her environment (Rutter 1991). Contexts such as home, community, schools and classrooms have been shown to provide protection to children and young people at risk and to direct their development towards positive and healthy pathways (Crosnoe and Elder 2004; Pianta and

Case study 2.1 A study of resilience

Emmy Werner and Ruth Smith began their pioneering longitudinal study on resilience back in 1963 and their study is still going on today. They began their investigation into the impact of social disadvantage on development over the lifespan among a group of 600 individuals living in Hawaii. All the participants were drawn from socio-economically impoverished backgrounds. At the age of 32, the majority (70%) had developed into healthy and successful young adults despite the high-risk environments in which they grew up. The study suggested that protective factors, both internal and external, had a stronger impact on children's developmental trajectory than risk factors. It identified three sets of factors that protected the individuals from the adverse effects of their negative life circumstances and directed their development towards more positive trajectories. These were: the dispositional attributes of the individual such as sociability and competence in communication skills; affectional ties within the family, providing emotional support in times of stress; and supportive and rewarding external support systems, such as school and work (Werner and Smith 1988, 1992).

Walsh 1998; Rees and Bailey 2003; Schoon 2006). Bronfenbrenner's (1979) ecological systems theory, with its representation of the developing individual embedded in a series of nested systems, provides a useful framework for analysing the dynamics of resilience-promoting contexts such as schools. Schools provide a major and continuing context for cognitive and socio-emotional development. They have significant and sustained contact with most children and young people during the formative years of personality development, and thus they can be ideal places for cognitive and socio-emotional development to be nurtured and supported. Rutter (1991) argues that the positive effects of school experience seem most evident among pupils who are vulnerable and have few other supports. Given that schools are one of the few institutions available to all children and young people, they are ideally placed to reach vulnerable pupils whom it may be difficult to access in other settings.

The resilience literature agrees on three key school qualities which have been found to promote positive academic and social outcomes, and compensate for risk factors such as socio-economic disadvantage (Benard 1991; Pianta and Walsh 1998; Rees and Bailey 2003):

1.   Caring relationships between pupils and teachers based on teacher concern, care, respect and support towards the pupils. An 'ethic of caring' (Noddings 1992) broadens such relationships beyond the classroom walls to include caring pupil–pupil, teacher–teacher and teacher–parent relationships.

2.   High expectations for pupils to do well through teacher practices which are child-centred, use pupils' own strengths and interests, and tap their intrinsic motivation for learning.

3.   Pupils' meaningful involvement and responsibility, with opportunities to express opinions, make choices, solve problems and work with and help others in a caring and healthy environment.

Table 2.1 at the end of the chapter presents a number of educational resilience studies that have examined the role of schools and classrooms as resilience-enhancing contexts for pupils coming from adverse social backgrounds.

RESILIENCE FOR ALL: A UNIVERSAL PERSPECTIVE

> Schools must do better for *all* our students…they all need to find and nurture relationships, see possibilities and potentials… [we need] to build a climate and a process within that climate that works to benefit all. (Brown *et al.* 2001, p.xi–xii)

Most of the current research on educational resilience has focused predominantly on academic success in the context of risk, particularly the achievement of pupils from minority, low-level socio-economic families and communities. There have been calls, however, to broaden the construct beyond this 'specifist' approach to include the wellbeing of all school children within a universal perspective of resilience (Battistisch 2001; Brown 2004; Carter and Doyle 2006; Cefai 2007; Poulou 2007). A universal approach to resilience focuses on common processes promoting positive academic and social behaviours among all pupils. Schools and classrooms are organised in such a way as to match the developmental needs of all their members, both those at risk and those who are not. Recent research suggests that factors which benefit children in adversity, such as caring and supportive relationships, an accessible and meaningful curriculum, and active participation in the classroom, have been found to benefit normally developing children as well (Solomon *et al.* 1997b, 2000). On the other hand, resilience builds upon typical psychosocial processes involved in the development of competence. The fundamental systems that generally foster competence in development, such as caring classroom relationships, positive academic beliefs and high expectations, operate in adverse circumstances as well, protecting the child or counteracting the threats to development (Masten and Coatsworth 1998; Rees and Bailey 2003). Another argument for a universal perspective is that cross-curricular and context-focused approaches appear to be more effective in promoting socio-emotional and academic competence than off-the-shelf intervention programmes targeting specific groups (Elias and Weissberg 2000; Pianta and Walsh 1998; Waxman et al. 2004). Programmes such as *Socio-Emotional Learning* in the USA (Elias and Weissberg 2000) and the *Social and Emotional Aspects of Learning* in the UK (Department for Education and Employment (DfEE) 2004) offer promising frameworks in this respect (Poulou 2007).

Within a universal model of resilience, schools and classrooms can adopt processes that will promote social and academic development among both at-risk pupils and those who are developing normally. These processes are grounded in the typical mechanisms involved in the development of social and academic competence. Caring classroom relationships, meaningful engagement, shared values and a sense of belonging have consistently been shown to be related to positive academic and social outcomes among pupils, including those considered at risk of school failure and psychosocial difficulties (Battistisch et al. 1995; Catalano and Hawkins 1996; Solomon et al. 1997a). Schools and classrooms are social systems with the potential to support the growth and wellbeing of all. They may provide a protective environment for vulnerable children and young people, while at the same time enhancing the development of the other normally developing pupils as well. This perspective avoids the differentiation and specialisation of support that may lead to further stress among vulnerable children (Pianta and Walsh 1998) and to the possibility of the stigmatisation and labelling of 'non-resilient' children (Waxman et al. 2004), with schools increasing risk rather than reducing it.

Most studies define the outcome of resilience as academic success on the basis of examination performance. However, there are technical and methodological problems in measuring school success solely on the basis of grades and tests. Even more problematic is the definition of educational resilience as academic achievement. Pupils may be achieving while at the same time facing considerable problems in social competence, problem solving and autonomous learning (Pianta and Walsh 1998). Moreover, such a definition provides a very limited view of what education is about, focusing on teaching and performance rather than on pupils and learning (Watkins 2001). It hinders the promotion of pupils' development as caring and responsible citizens (Nicholls 1989) and as competent, self-directed learners (Watkins et al. 2002). It also makes it impossible for a substantial number of pupils to succeed and be 'resilient'.

With this in mind, educational resilience in this book is defined as 'socio-emotional competence and educational engagement in the classroom'.

Educational engagement is based on Newman, Wehlage and Lamborn's (1992) term 'student engagement' and refers to positive academic attitudes, motivation to achieve and to learn, and enjoyment of class and school. Socio-emotional competence, on the other hand, generally refers to the social and communicative skills children use to cultivate relationships with adults and peers to succeed in an environment. These include helping and working collaboratively with peers, autonomy and problem-solving skills. This ability is usually defined in terms of age-appropriate skills within socially relevant contexts. There appears to be some broad consensus of what constitutes desirable behaviours, such as establishing and maintaining a range of positive social behaviours, refraining from harming others, contributing collaboratively to peer group and school, engaging in behaviours which enhance and protect health, and avoiding behaviours with serious negative consequences for the individual or others or both (Topping, Bremner and Holmes 2000)

Educational resilience in this book is construed as a dynamic, contextual phenomenon rather than a fixed, individual characteristic. In this respect, it can be built and enhanced within the contexts in which children and young people operate, such as the classroom. The definition is positive and inclusive, it focuses on learning rather than achievement, and is open to all rather than limited to a select few. It is global and holistic, focusing both on the cognitive and on the affective elements of children's and young people's development. It has also a proactive, universal dimension, moving away from risk towards classrooms operating as health-promoting and competence-enhancing contexts for all their pupils.

CONCLUSION

The universal approach to resilience suggested in this book does not seek to realign the construct towards the general pupil population while ignoring or excluding tried-and-tested interventions focused on pupils considered at risk. Rather, it suggests broadening the construct to include a parallel (and complementary) generalist perspective which focuses on common pathways to foster competence among all children and young people in school. In this book, the term 'educational resilience' is used within this universal perspective. It is not concerned with how schools and classrooms may prevent failure and dysfunction among vulnerable children, but with how they may promote the healthy development of all children, including those coming from adverse circumstances. It underlines the need to focus on common and inclusive contextual processes and interventions.

Points for reflection

1. Compare and contrast the risk and resilience perspectives in education. In what way does resilience provide a more positive and proactive view of children's and young people's development?

2. The resilience perspective suggests that we may be more effective in supporting children's and young people's development and wellbeing by focusing on their strengths than on their weaknesses. How true is this for the classroom practitioner?

3. What are your views on the universal approach to educational resilience proposed in this chapter? What are the implications of this approach for classroom teaching and learning?

SUMMARY

- Earlier approaches to school success and failure have been dominated by the risk model, which sought to prevent or remedy failure among pupils coming from adverse circumstances.

- The failure of the risk model to explain success and failure at school adequately led to a paradigm shift towards resilience- and competence-enhancement models of development. The resilience perspective shifted the focus from deficit towards growth, seeking to explain what makes children at risk achieve and be successful at school. It suggests that we may be more effective in supporting children's and young people's development by focusing on their strengths rather than on their weaknesses.

- Three sets of protective factors have been identified as providing protection to children and young people at risk, namely the dispositional attributes of the individual, the family and external support systems such as the school.

- The literature converges on three qualities of schools and classrooms which operate as resilience-enhancing contexts: namely, caring relationships, meaningful engagement and high expectations.

- The universal model of resilience in this book proposes that resilience building in the classroom can occur through common processes that promote positive social and academic behaviour among normally developing children and young people as well as those who may be at risk in their development. It is not concerned with how schools and classrooms may prevent failure among vulnerable children, but with how they may promote educational engagement and socio-emotional competence among all pupils. Educational resilience in this book is defined as pupils' educational engagement and socio-emotional competence.

Table 2.1: Key studies in educational resilience

Study	Description
Rutter et al. (1979)	This study of 12 Inner London comprehensive schools was one of the first to suggest that schools are an important source of external protective factors for children considered at risk. Students coming from disadvantaged or problematic families were more likely to demonstrate resilient characteristics if they attended schools with a positive ethos such as an academic pressure and high expectations, attentive and caring teachers, and good teacher–student relationships.
Wehlage et al. (1989)	A study of 14 high schools that have been successful with at-risk children in terms of increased literacy performance and school attendance. Students who identified themselves with the mainstream school culture and had established a social bond with peers and adults in the school were less likely to disengage and more likely to participate in the life of the school and to achieve. The successful schools were notable for a teacher culture characterised by a moral obligation to serve young people.
Wang, Haertel and Walberg (1993)	This research synthesis identified a consistent pattern of organisational and behavioural characteristics among inner-city schools that promoted educational resilience among students at risk. Teacher actions and expectations, and effective instructional methods and curriculum, played key roles in pupil motivation, positive attitude towards school, achievement and prosocial behaviour. Teachers' concern and sustained close relationships with pupils, the high expectations for all pupils, tailoring of instructions to meet the needs of individual pupils, engaging pupils in setting goals and making learning decisions, shared interests and values, a high degree of engagement and pupil satisfaction with learning experiences were consistently associated with enhanced pupil cognitive and affective outcomes.
Freiberg, Stein and Huang (1995)	A study in a number of inner-city elementary schools in the USA. Classroom management, based on pupil ownership and responsibility, with teachers and pupils working collaboratively to create opportunities for self-discipline, was related to higher rates of engagement and achievement, more positive attitudes towards school, and fewer behaviour problems. An in-depth study of one of the schools, a predominantly African-American school which previously had the lowest achievement record in the district, identified active pupil involvement, supportive administration, celebration of success, a sense of belonging, supporting pupils in need and parental involvement as key factors contributing to pupil resilience.

Resnick et al. (1997)	An analysis of the *Minnesota Adolescent Health Survey*, a large database from a state-wide survey of over 36,000 seventh to twelfth grade students, revealed that the experience of being catered for and the feeling of connectedness resulted in demonstrably greater wellbeing and correspondingly less risky, health-compromising behaviours among students in general, particularly those considered 'at risk'. School connectedness was the most important protective factor for students against antisocial behaviour.
Waxman, Huang and Wang (1997a, 1997b); Padron, Waxman and Huang (1999)	Hersch Waxman and his colleagues carried out a number of studies on the achievement of elementary and middle school pupils coming from low socio-economic urban minorities in the USA. They found that, in contrast to their low-achieving peers, high-achieving pupils reported more positive views of their educational experiences, involvement and aspirations, were more engaged in the classroom activities, and viewed their teachers as supportive and encouraging.
Hawkins et al. (1999)	A longitudinal study which sought to promote pupils' academic and social competence and connectedness to school in a number of primary schools serving high-crime areas. It reported greater pupil commitment and attachment to school, less misbehaviour and better academic achievement, particularly among pupils coming from poorer families, in the schools following the intervention programme.
Criss et al. (2002)	A longitudinal study on the relationship between family adversity, positive peer relationships and children's externalising behaviour with 600 young children who experienced adverse family situations in three different sites in the USA. Children's peer acceptance and friendships at school moderated the effects of family adversity, protecting children from antisocial and aggressive behaviours.
Solomon et al. (1997a/1997b, 2000)	The Child Development Programme (CDP) sought to build a sense of caring community in schools. Pupils attending the CDP schools scored significantly higher on outcomes such as general social competence, conflict resolution, empathy and self-esteem, and school-related variables such as liking for school, achievement motivation and reading comprehension. Teacher practices that encouraged pupils' active participation, collaboration and interpersonal support through an emphasis on prosocial values, eliciting of pupils' own thinking and ideas and encouragement of cooperation and supportiveness were related to pupil engagement, influence and positive behaviour. These findings held for a broad variety of pupils including pupils from low socio-economic status, urban areas and ethnic minorities.

FURTHER READING

Battistisch, V., Solomon, D., Dong-il, K., Watson, M. and Schaps, E. (1995) 'Schools as communities, poverty levels of student populations, and students' attitudes, motives and performance: a multilevel analysis.' *American Educational Research Journal 32*, 627–658.

Brown, J.H., D'Emidio-Caston, M. and Benard, B. (2001) *Resilience Education*. Thousand Oaks, CA: Corwin Press.

Cefai, C. (Guest Editor) 'Emotional Behaviour Difficulties'. *Special Edition on Educational Resilience, 12,* 2, June 2007, 87–162.

Pianta, R.C. and Walsh, D.J. (1998) 'Applying the construct of resilience in schools: cautions from a developmental systems perspective.' *School Psychology Review 27*, 3, 407–417.

Waxman, H.C., Gray, J.P. and Padron, Y.N. (2003) *Review of Research on Educational Resilience*. Centre for Research on Education, Diversity & Excellence, University of California, Santa Cruz. Available at www.cal.org/crede/pubs/research/RR11.pdf) (accessed 12 December 2007).

Waxman, H.C., Padron, N.Y. and Chang, H. (eds) (2004) *Educational Resiliency: Student, Teacher, and School Perspectives*. Connecticut: Information Age Publishing.

Werner, E. and Smith, R. (1992) *Overcoming the Odds: High-Risk Children from Birth to Adulthood*. New York: Cornell University Press.

CHAPTER 3

A Model of Resilience-enhancing Classrooms

This chapter presents a theoretical model of educational resilience within a universal perspective, with classrooms operating as resilience-enhancing contexts for all their pupils. The chapter first describes how the model was developed from the study of a number of classrooms, making use of two converging bodies of literature, namely educational resilience and caring classrooms. This is then followed by a detailed description of the model of classrooms as caring, inclusive, prosocial and learning-centred communities. The final section explains how the classrooms described in the model may contribute to educational engagement and socio-emotional competence among the pupils through the satisfaction of children's basic psychological needs.

There are numerous ready-made programmes for the promotion of educational resilience in schools. Many of these programmes, however, particularly the off-the-shelf ones, have largely been ineffective in bringing about change in children's lives in the long term (Pianta and Walsh 1998). Programmes based on lists of protective characteristics and distinct formulas that are promoted as being applicable across different cultures and contexts are fraught with difficulties. Schools and classrooms are complex social systems and any explanations of how they promote resilience and competence would have to be as complex as the contexts themselves. Systemic interventions require reflexivity, with the persons intervening locating themselves in relation to the process of change taking place within that particular context. This requires types of self-analysis and reflection that off-the-shelf packages actually inhibit.

Schools need to be particularly cautious in adopting approaches that have proven successful in other countries [with] different cultural and

> educational backgrounds…US programmes are…often too pre-planned, top-down and normative to be usable in European context[s] without careful adaptation. (Weare 2000, p.36)

> As we move from a study of inputs and outputs to a more integrated notion of classroom processes, we need to ask different questions using contextualised theories and methods. (Turner and Meyer 2000, p.71)

The model presented in this book seeks to avoid the traps of the quick-fix syndrome and to appreciate the complexity of the phenomena and contexts being examined. It has been developed from a naturalistic study of classrooms, through an active engagement with the classroom participants themselves.[1] The insights developed from the extended study of a small number of primary school classrooms were linked with the existing theory to develop a model of how classrooms can become resilience-enhancing contexts. The model is situated in Bronfenbrenner's systems theory of development and draws on two converging bodies of literature, educational resilience and caring school communities, in proposing a universal model of educational resilience. The following sections describe the development and workings of the model in more detail.

CARING COMMUNITIES

The resilience literature has identified caring relationships between pupils and teachers, pupil engagement in meaningful activities and high expectations as the key resilient factors in schools (Rees and Bailey 2003; Resnick *et al.* 1997; Rutter 1990; Werner and Smith 1988). The presence of caring and nurturing relationships between pupils and teachers is one of the most commonly identified protective factors. Child competence, particularly up to the late primary school period, is often embedded in the relationships with adults. These relationships provide high 'affordance' for the processes that promote positive outcomes and compensate for risk factors such as socio-economic disadvantage or problematic relationships with parents (Lynch and Cicchetti 1992; Pianta 1999). The sense of connectedness (the experience of caring and a sense of closeness to school staff and the environment) generated by such relationships helps to create an atmosphere which promotes learning and social competence. Meaningful pupil involvement and responsibility, such as the opportunity to express opinions, make choices, solve problems and work with and help others, is another key factor identified by the literature as promoting educational resilience. Finally,

1   More details on how the study was carried out may be found in the Appendix.

resilience-promoting schools and classrooms set high expectations for pupils to do well, with classroom practices using pupils' own strengths and goals and tapping into their intrinsic motivation for learning (Battistisch, Solomon and Delucchi 1993; Freiberg *et al.* 1995; Waxman *et al.* 1997a, 1997b).

The educational resilience literature converges with that on school community in the study of the impact of the caring classroom community on learning and behaviour. The importance of community building as a basis for learning was advocated almost a century ago by John Dewey, who wrote extensively on the relational and interpersonal aspect of education. More recently other researchers and educationalists have underlined the contribution of caring school communities to pupils' learning and social competence (e.g. Battistisch *et al.* 1995; Bryk and Driscoll 1988; Sergiovanni 1994). Caring communities are defined by their caring relationships, active and influential participation, and shared beliefs and goals. Community members share a sense of belonging and are committed to common goals and values. They care about each other, work together collaboratively and are actively engaged in the life of the community. This sense of belonging applies to all, with no individual or group of individuals being left out. The community broadcasts the belief that all members can be successful in their learning, and provides opportunities and resources so that all pupils can participate and succeed. Collaboration and cohesiveness are promoted within an inclusive framework, with all pupils being positively engaged (Anderman 2002). Finally, classroom communities promoting competence and resilience share values and norms focused on pupils' wellbeing and learning and on prosocial values and behaviours.

> Shared beliefs in…getting people together and acting in concert…in ensuring that marginalized voices are heard, are important not only for the fact that they are shared, but also that they reflect ideals of participation and egalitarian communities. (Westheimer 1998, p.142)

When pupils perceive their classroom focus as one of learning rather than performance, on improving rather than proving competence, on sharing and supporting each other, they are more likely to feel connected to their group, to become engaged in the classroom activities, and consequently improve their learning and behaviour (Battistisch *et al.* 1997).

Caring communities are related to a number of positive cognitive and social outcomes. Pupils with a sense of community are more likely to develop positive academic attitudes and behaviours. They participate in learning and other activities, engage in prosocial and collaborative behaviour, and have a sense of competence and responsibility (Battistisch *et al.* 1997; Solomon *et al.* 1992; Wang and Haertel 1995). This is evident for both normally developing pupils as well as those who are vulnerable in their learning and behaviour (Battistisch *et al.* 1995; Solomon *et al.* 2000). In an evaluation study in five elementary schools in the USA, Solomon *et al.* (2000) reported that the schools operating as caring communities showed gains, relative to the control schools, in pupils' motivation and engagement, personal and interpersonal concerns and skills, and prosocial values and behaviours. On the other hand, schools that emphasised the assessment of traditional goals with standardised achievement tests showed little gains in academic achievement. Significant effects held for a broad variety of pupils, including those from low socio-economic groups, urban areas and ethnic minorities. In another evaluation study in 24 diverse elementary schools, Battistisch *et al.* (1997) reported that a sense of community was related to a large number of positive pupil attitudes, motivational orientations and prosocial behaviours. It was found to be particularly beneficial for pupils considered at risk.

THE CLASSROOM AS THE ARENA FOR CHANGE

> All the evidence that has been generated in the school effectiveness research community shows that classrooms are far more important than schools in determining how children perform at school. (Muijs and Reynolds 2001, p.vii)

Schools are social systems functioning at various levels, with each layer carrying its own distinctive characteristic and having the potential to impact on pupil behaviour (cf. Bronfenbrenner 1989). While there are indications that the school and classroom layers are more likely to be related and to support one another (Crone and Teddlie 1995; Kyriakides, Campbell and Gagatsis 2000), such coincidence should not be assumed to be automatic. The classroom is an important context in children's development and influences their learning, performance and social competence. Research suggests that its influence on learning and behaviour may be stronger than that of the school layer (Brown, Riddell and Duffield 1996; Kyriakides *et al.* 2000). Classroom climate studies have demonstrated that, when pupils feel accepted and supported in the classroom, they are more likely to become engaged in activities and to interact prosocially with their peers (Fraser 1994; Johnson, Johnson and Stanne 2000; Slavin 1991). Motivational literature similarly suggests that classroom processes, such as perceived teacher support and pupil involvement, affect pupils' motivation and engagement in learning and have more influence than processes outside the classroom (Gurtner, Monnard and Genoud 2001). Finally, the literature on caring classroom communities suggests that pupils' sense of classroom community is related positively to their motivation, learning and behaviour (Battistisch *et al.* 1995; Connell and Wellborn 1991;

Goodenow 1993): pupils are more likely to develop positive attitudes towards school and learning, become actively engaged in the learning process and engage in prosocial and collaborative behaviour with peers. This holds good regardless of the pupils' backgrounds; indeed, the influence of a caring community may be even more beneficial for the pupils coming from disadvantaged backgrounds (Battistisch et al. 1995; Solomon et al. 1997a, 1997b).

The classroom is at the centre of the model presented in this chapter. It is the arena where caring relationships and meaningful engagement are particularly set to take place and where pupils are more likely to have opportunities to develop closer relationships with their teachers and with their peers, to help each other, to work and learn together, to share responsibility and to participate actively in meaningful activities. While they may participate in whole-school activities, their interactions, engagement and relationships within this layer are likely to be relatively weaker and less frequent. This suggests that pupils' sense of classroom belonging is likely to be stronger than that of school belonging, and that the former is more likely to influence pupils' behaviour than the latter.

While examining the classroom processes, however, one must be careful not to commit the same mistake as the previous studies that focused exclusively on the school as an organisation. Processes occurring at the school level influence what happens in the classroom as well. McLaughlin's (1993) three-year study on professional community in schools found that the quality of the teachers' professional community had a significant impact on how they responded to pupils in their classrooms. Teachers who worked in collaborative, collegial and cohesive schools or departments were more innovative in their work, more energetic and enthusiastic, and more open to personal and professional development. They were also more committed to addressing pupils' needs and supporting their learning. Clearly teachers with a sense of belonging are more likely to be committed and engaged in their work and to express and provide care and support to their pupils. Sergiovanni (1996) underlines the need to acknowledge the link between what happens to teachers and what happens to students: 'the idea of making classrooms into learning communities for students will remain more rhetoric than real unless schools also become learning communities for teachers' (p.42).

The following section describes in detail the model of classrooms as resilience-enhancing contexts and how it works in promoting socio-emotional competence and educational engagement for pupils in the classroom.

A MODEL OF CLASSROOMS AS RESILIENCE-ENHANCING CONTEXTS

Figure 3.1 presents a model of classrooms as caring, inclusive, prosocial and learning-centred communities, promoting educational engagement and socio-emotional competence in all pupils, including vulnerable ones. The model consists of three connected elements: the processes characterising the classroom contexts; the contextual forces facilitating these processes; and the outcomes of these processes in terms of pupil resilience. It suggests theoretical links between the processes, facilitating forces and outcomes.

The processes reflect three major areas of classroom practice, namely relationships (caring relationships among the classroom members), engagement (authentic, inclusive, collaborative and influential engagement) and shared beliefs and values (a shared focus on learning, learning together, learning for all and prosocial values) (see Figure 3.2). They are facilitated by contextual forces both within the classroom and the school, as well as by outside school forces such as parents, the local community and the national educational community. The classroom and school levels are construed as two connected but differentiated systems, with classrooms having a stronger influence on behaviour. The influences of classroom and school processes are reciprocal, and when the two contexts coincide, as they are likely to do when they operate as the kind of community proposed by this model, they have an additional, complementary effect on pupil behaviour. The final section of the model makes use of existing theory to explain how the classroom community is related to educational resilience as defined in this book. With its many interconnections, the model reflects the complexity of the classroom context itself. It seeks to avoid simplistic and mechanical explanations and is built on reciprocal and circular criteria. While processes taking place in the classroom contribute to pupil resilience, for instance, the processes themselves are influenced by the actual practice of resilient behaviour. The following describes in more detail the various elements of the model.

Classroom processes and facilitating forces

Classroom contexts marked by educational engagement and socio-emotional competence operate as caring, inclusive, prosocial and learning-centred communities. Members feel connected and supported, are meaningfully and influentially engaged in activities and provided with opportunities to be successful, competent and autonomous, to work together collaboratively and to share a common focus on learning and prosocial behaviour. These processes and the way they are facilitated by classroom and out-of-classroom/school contextual forces are discussed in the following.

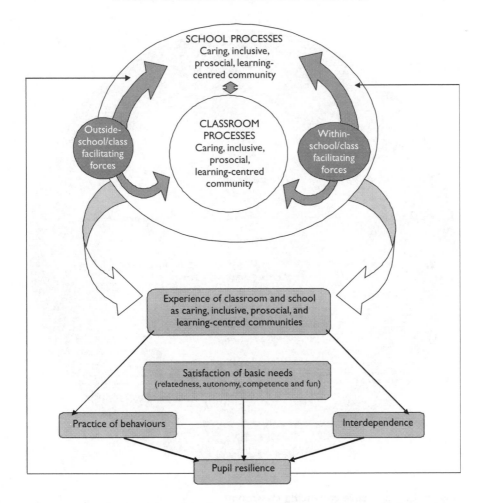

Figure 3.1: A theoretical model of resilience-enhancing classroom and school contexts

Caring and connecting classrooms

Relationships are the hallmark of caring communities. Teachers and pupils and the pupils themselves are connected to each other, forming part of a 'common house of belonging'. Pupils feel safe, valued and trusted. They are supported in their learning and are encouraged to support each other. Teachers take on a dual role as effective and nurturing educators, supporting pupils' learning and academic success, while seeking to address their socio-affective needs. They appreciate the need to know the pupils well and to adapt their methods according to their needs. They reach out to their pupils, showing interest and respect, listening to their stories and concerns, expressing warmth and affection, and providing nurture and

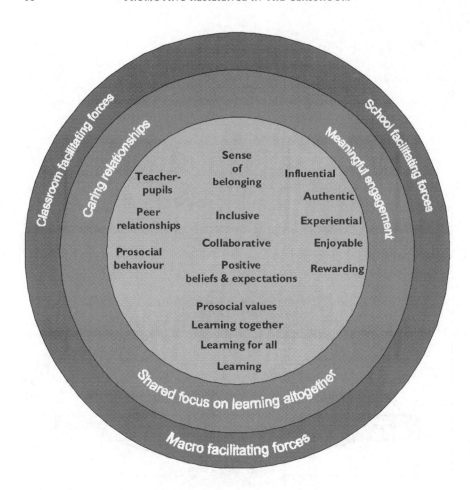

Figure 3.2: Resilience-enhancing classrooms

support. They invest heavily in building relationships and in creating teaching and learning experiences within a culture of care. They become engaged in mutual and reciprocal interactions with their pupils. Their practice influences their pupils' behaviour and is in turn influenced by it. Being loved, valued and looked up to feeds into teachers' own needs for affiliation, esteem and generativity, and teachers are more likely to respond with similar behaviour towards their pupils. The school climate, staff relationships and relationships with parents are other important influences on classroom relationships.

Prosocial and supportive classrooms

Care, solidarity, collaboration, acceptance and celebration of diversity are the key values underlining pupil behaviour in the classroom. Pupils care for and support each other, and work and play together. They solve conflicts amicably and constructively. Instead of competing with each other, they help each other with their work. Supporting one another is a celebrated classroom value. Practices which help to foster these behaviours include: socio-emotional literacy training; structured and incidental teaching on what is appropriate and inappropriate classroom behaviour; reinforcement of prosocial behaviours and discouragement of antisocial and competitive behaviours; and opportunities to practise these social competence and engagement skills. Through their own practice and behaviour with pupils and with other adults in the classroom, teachers also act as role models of these types of behaviour. Similarly, the peer group's encouragement and role modelling of prosocial behaviours, and discouragement and rejection of negative ones, encourages pupils to learn together and thrive without fear. Factors outside the classroom, such as staff and pupil relationships at the school level, parental influence, school policies and socio-cultural values, also contribute to pupils' relationships and prosocial behaviour in the classroom.

Engaging classrooms

Pupils are provided with opportunities for real engagement in the classroom activities. They participate actively and enthusiastically in experiential and meaningful activities that make use of pupil-centred and activity-based instructional strategies connected to the pupils' own life experiences. Learning is an enjoyable, inherently motivating, authentic enterprise. The focus should be on learning rather than performance, away from the excessive emphasis on academic pressure and examinations. The celebration of the pupils' and group's achievements and efforts is a common practice. Instructional practices that help to create an engaging classroom context include experiential learning, use of resources and interactive activities, and a pedagogy drawing on pupils' own developmental stages, experiences and interests. Rewarding experiences are also likely to connect pupils to the contexts where those experiences take place and to the people who instigate, contribute or share the experiences. Teachers' own motivation and enthusiasm, and their care and support, make participation not only a rewarding experience, but also a desirable enterprise.

Inclusive classrooms: engagement and learning for all

All pupils are included in the academic and social activities taking place in the classroom. Classroom membership is open to all pupils irrespective of any difference in ability, background or interest. All pupils feel an important part of the community. They have the opportunity to participate in the activities and to be successful in their learning. Pupils in difficulty are considered an important asset for the group rather than a liability. Support is made available to pupils with learning, social, behavioural and emotional difficulties through individual attention, peer support and additional support. Teachers encourage the practice of accepting, respecting and helping each other and frequently act as role models for such behaviours themselves. School-level policies and practices, macro-level influences such as national policies on social inclusion and cultural values promoting acceptance and solidarity are other contextual forces contributing to the creation of inclusive classrooms.

Collaborative classrooms

Pupils are supported to work collaboratively and construct learning experiences together. They do not compete with each other and do not need to measure their learning and achievement against those of their peers. Teachers themselves work collaboratively and collegially with other adults in the classroom, sharing practice and providing mutual support. Parents engage in a collaborative relationship with the teachers in supporting their children's learning. Pupil collaboration is facilitated by opportunities to learn together and from each other. The physical setting, with pupils sitting in groups and facing each other and with space to move around, encourages pupils to interact and work together. The use of small group work and pair work, the recognition and celebration of the group's efforts and achievements, the discouragement of competition, the emphasis on learning for all and the teamwork between the class teacher and other members of staff are other contextual forces promoting collective and interdependent communities. The staff's own collegiality and collaboration, a whole-school focus on learning together and parents' involvement in the school, as well as broader educational and socio-cultural influences, all help to promote a culture of learning together.

Empowering classrooms

Pupils are provided with opportunities where they can be influential and autonomous. They are listened to and consulted on classroom activities and behaviours, given choices and autonomy in their work, and valued as learners and individuals through recognition, positive beliefs and high expectations. Teachers believe that all pupils can learn if they work hard enough. They communicate these positive beliefs and expectations through their own commitment and enthusiasm, their affirmation of pupils' abilities and successes, their expectations that pupils are to work harder and achieve more, and their attending to pupils in their work.

Opportunities and encouragement for pupils to make choices on what to learn and how to behave, to be less dependent on the teacher in their work and to find their own solutions to difficulties and conflicts support the pupils' basic need for autonomy. The recognition of pupils' efforts and achievements, the promotion of their academic and non-academic strengths and the opportunity to be successful help to affirm pupils' belief in themselves and their group and to promote their engagement in classroom activities. Teachers' belief in themselves as professionals and in being able to make a difference in the life of the group also contribute to the creation of an enabling context for the pupils. Positive beliefs, high expectations and recognition by peers, the administration and parents are other forces likely to help in empowering classrooms.

Learning-focused classrooms

Classroom members share common purposes and values related to learning, learning for all, learning together and prosocial behaviour. The classroom has a common focus on learning rather than merely on performance, on learning for all rather than for those who are able to do so without support, on learning with rather than against each other and on engaging in prosocial behaviour. This collective focus serves to connect the members together in striving to reach their common goals. Some of the contextual factors which help to instil this shared focus include: explicit teaching and story-telling by classroom teachers and other members of staff; reinforcement and public recognition of desirable behaviours and discouragement of inappropriate ones; role modelling by peers, teachers and staff; parental support; and opportunities to practise behaviours resulting from these shared values.

Classroom processes and pupil outcomes

The seven classroom processes described above, supported by the respective facilitating forces, help to bring members together and to increase mutuality, shared responsibility and interdependence. They serve as a source of sustenance for the functioning of the classroom as a caring community and, consequently, create a climate conducive to engagement and socio-emotional competence. When pupils experience contexts operating as caring and inclusive communities focused on learning and prosocial values, their four basic needs for relatedness, competence, autonomy and fun are satisfied. They feel safe and secure, connected and included, valued and supported, influential and autonomous, recognized and competent. As pupils experience contexts where they

- feel connected with their teacher and their peers

- are told that what they do is valid and worthwhile and that they can improve their learning and performance

- are supported to engage in meaningful activities in which they feel autonomous and successful

- see their accomplishments and efforts recognised and celebrated

- have their voice heard and their choices respected

- share common values and beliefs related to learning all together cooperatively

- work together collaboratively to achieve common goals

they develop a sense of classroom belonging and become more willing to engage in academic and social behaviours informed by the classroom's norms and values. Once engaged, they are more likely to perceive their classroom as attractive, to show more interest in learning and to experience success in learning and achievement. As they do so, they develop a sense of control and efficacy, and consequently are more likely to engage in similar behaviours in the future. The group itself becomes a powerful medium for the sustenance and maintenance of such behaviours. Pupils in these communities, including pupils who may be at risk in one or more area of their development, are consequently set to engage in the following behaviours:

- motivation and engagement, and consequently success, in learning

- prosocial, caring and supportive behaviours, such as caring for each other, sharing with others and showing understanding, respect and concern

- collective orientation favouring collaboration, working and learning together, helping others in their work and avoiding competition and conflict in seeking achievement

- taking responsibility for their own and their peers' learning.

ADDRESSING PUPILS' BASIC PSYCHOLOGICAL NEEDS

The self-determination theory (Deci *et al.* 1991) provides a theoretical basis for the link between the classroom contexts as proposed in this model and pupils' educational engagement and socio-emotional competence. Classrooms operating as caring, inclusive, prosocial and learning-centred communities address the fundamental psychological needs of children and young people. The satisfaction of the need for relatedness, competence, autonomy and fun contributes to pupils' active engagement in the learning process and in the life of the classroom, which in turn leads to learning, achievement and socio-emotional competence (Connell and Wellborn 1991; Deci and Ryan 1995).

First, pupils experiencing a caring classroom community develop a sense of affiliation to their teacher and to their group. Being close to each other and feeling valued and cared for promotes a sense of interconnectedness and belonging, one of the basic psychological needs of children and young people (Glaser 1990). Second, when pupils feel engaged, included and recognised, their sense of self-worth and competence, both as persons and as learners, is enhanced. Such an experience satisfies their need for personal power and competence. Third, when they believe they have choices in their learning and a say in decisions, pupils' need for personal freedom and autonomy is satisfied. Finally, a sense of enjoyment and adventure when engaged in experiential and stimulating classroom activities and in healthy relationships fulfils pupils' need for fun (Glaser 1990).

Pupils who have their fundamental needs satisfied are strongly motivated to engage in the positive academic and social behaviours being promoted and practised in the classroom. They are more likely to respect and care for their peers and their teachers, to support each other in their work and in times of need, to share and learn together, to recognise and value others, and to include others in their play and in their work. They are also likely to develop positive attitudes towards learning, becoming more committed, enthusiastic and self-reliant. As they establish a sense of belonging to the classroom context and its norms and values, they are more likely to care about and practise those values, not because of extrinsic motivators, pressure or coercion, but because they want to (Battistisch *et al.* 1995; Deci and Ryan 1985).

Relatedness, autonomy, competence and fun are integrated and complementary, and the satisfaction of one need supports the others (Ryan 1995). When pupils are provided with opportunities to be autonomous, their relationships with significant adults are strengthened (Wentzel 1997; Wentzel and Asher 1995). On the other hand, autonomy and competence develop more effectively in situations where children feel a sense of connectedness and relatedness to significant adults (Ryan 1995; Ryan and Powelson 1991). Generally, however, schools and classrooms are more likely to focus on the need for competence while ignoring the others, particularly the need for relatedness and autonomy (Osterman 2000). This is particularly true in contexts where the most important currency is that of performance and examinations. In such instances the classroom is unlikely to operate as a resilience-enhancing context. Lack of pupil autonomy in the classroom, for instance, is related to negative academic and social behaviour such as competition and lack of support (Manke 1997; Solomon *et al.* 1997a). Similarly, schools and classrooms that are perceived as unsupportive with poor relationships among their members have relatively high levels of stress, disaffection and absenteeism among staff and pupils (Kyriacu 1996; Moos 1991).

The self-efficacy theory (Bandura 1993, 1997) provides further insight into how the classroom context described above contributes to educational resilience. Pupils who experience classrooms as caring, inclusive, prosocial and learning-centred communities become engaged in the learning and social experiences promoted within those classrooms. Consequently, they are likely to enter into a virtuous cycle where the actual practice of behaviour encourages similar behaviours in the future. They become more confident in their own competencies and those of others, experience a positive social and academic esteem and efficacy, both personal and collective, and believe more in themselves and others as worthy persons and learners. As a result of their individual and collective sense of efficacy, they are more likely to participate actively in classroom activities, to persist in the face of difficulty, to deal more effectively and constructively with problem situations, and to engage in more prosocial behaviour (Bandura 1993; Linnenbrink and Pintrich 2003). This is true of all pupils in the classroom, including pupils coming from socially disadvantaged backgrounds (Battistisch *et al.* 1995; Wang and Haertel 1995). Clearly, classrooms are created and shaped by the very behaviours they influence.

Finally, in line with the multilayered model of schools suggested in this model (Bronfenbrenner 1989),staff relationships are also set to impact on pupils' behaviour in the classroom. Staff's own sense of belonging and community has a positive, added impact on pupils' learning and behaviour (Bryk and Driscoll 1988; Bryk, Camburn and Louis 1999). Collegiality, collaboration, engagement and shared values and beliefs contribute to a sense of belonging among the staff. This feeds back into the processes occurring at both school and classroom levels, as staff become more likely to share the school's values, vision and objectives, and to contribute towards the realisation of those objectives in the classroom. They work more effectively, are more committed to addressing pupils' needs and putting more effort into creating and sustaining opportunities for pupil learning (McLaughlin 1993; McLaughlin and Talbert 2006). When teachers' own interpersonal needs are addressed, they are more likely to pay more attention to the personal needs of their own pupils (Pianta 1997).

CONCLUSION

The classroom processes described in this model have been developed from the study of a number of classrooms characterised by educational engagement and socio-emotional competence. The second part of the book presents various por-traits of these processes, providing illustrations from real classrooms. It serves to ground the theoretical model presented here in actual classroom practice. The following five chapters touch on the various aspects of the classroom relationships and engagement described in the model, namely: *caring classrooms* (teacher–pupil relationships); *prosocial classrooms* (peer relationships and pupil behaviour); *engaging classrooms* (authentic and inclusive engagement); *collaborative classrooms* (cooperative learning, staff collaboration, teacher–parent collaboration); and *empowering classrooms* (voice, choice and positive beliefs and expectations). The learning-focused classrooms process overlaps with the other processes and has thus been included in the other five chapters to avoid repetition.

Points for reflection

1. As a classroom practitioner you may have developed your own theory of what helps children to engage in learning and prosocial behaviour in the classroom. How does your own model compare with the one presented in this chapter? What are the points of convergence and divergence?

2. The model in this chapter proposes seven key processes characterising resilience-enhancing classrooms. How do the classrooms portrayed here compare with your own actual experience as a classroom practitioner? To what extent do you think that these are practical processes which may be facilitated in the actual classroom?

SUMMARY

-   The universal resilience model suggests that educational resilience for all pupils is encouraged when classrooms are organised as caring, inclusive, prosocial and learning-centred communities.

-   The model was developed from the study of primary school classrooms in conjunction with existing knowledge in the area. It draws on two converging lines of research, namely educational resilience and caring communities.

-   Schools can be seen as multilayered systems, with classrooms having a distinct, direct and stronger impact on pupil behaviour.

-   The model consists of three connected elements: the key classroom processes; the contextual forces facilitating these processes; and the outcome of these processes in terms of pupil resilience.

- Three areas of classroom practice define the processes, namely caring relationships, authentic, inclusive, collaborative and influential engagement, and a shared focus on learning and prosocial values.

- Seven key processes with accompanying contextual forces are presented, namely caring classrooms, prosocial classrooms, engaging classrooms, inclusive classrooms, collaborative classrooms, empowering classrooms and learning-focused classrooms.

- The self-determination theory (Deci *et al.* 1991) together with the theory of self-efficacy (Bandura 1997) provide the basis for the link between the classroom contexts as proposed in this model and pupils' outcome. Pupils' resilience is explained by the extent to which their psychological needs are supported and satisfied in the classroom.

FURTHER READING

Battistisch, V., Watson, M., Solomon, D., Lewis, C. and Schaps, E. (1999) 'Beyond the three R's: a broader agenda for school reform.' *The Elementary School Journal 99*, 5, 414–432.

Bluestein, J. (2001) *Creating Emotionally Safe Schools: A Guide for Educators and Parents.* Deerfield Beach, FL: Health Communication Inc.

Bronfenbrenner, U. (1989) 'Ecological systems theory.' *Annals of Child Development 6*, 187–249.

Cohen, J. (ed.) (2001) *Caring Classrooms / Intelligent Schools: The Social Emotional Education of Young Children.* New York: Teachers College Press.

Deci, E.L., Vallerand, R.J., Pelleiter, L.G. and Ryan, R.M. (1991) 'Motivation and education: the self determination perspective.' *Educational Psychologist 26*, 325–346.

Osterman, F.K. (2000) 'Students' need for belonging in the school community.' *Review of Educational Research 70*, 323–367.

Sergiovanni, T.J. (1994) *Building School Communities.* San Francisco: Jossey-Bass Publications.

Solomon, D., Watson, M., Battistisch, V., Schaps, E. and Delucchi, K. (1997) 'Creating classrooms that students experience as communities.' *American Journal of Community Psychology, 24*, 6, 719–748.

Watkins, C. (2005) *Classrooms as Learning Communities: What's In It For Schools?* Oxford: Routledge.

PART 2

CLASSROOM PRACTICE

Much of the material in this book was developed from the findings of a revealing study of classrooms. The nine classes in the study were selected for their high level of pupil resilience (educational engagement and socio-emotional competence), thus serving as models of good practice in resilience enhancement.[1] Reading the narratives, accounts and stories in the following chapters, one might be tempted to think these are idealised classrooms which practitioners are unlikely to come across in real life. In fact, although chosen as models of good practice, these classrooms had their own problems and concerns, like all other social systems. The aim of the research was, however, to illuminate processes from which one could learn most about resilience enhancement, and accordingly the 'spotlight' was directed towards those processes. As Westheimer (1998, p.23) aptly puts it: '...when researchers observe any event, they are, in effect, shining a spotlight on their area of inquiry and simultaneously darkening all others; the circle of light that is cast both illuminates the interior and eclipses all that falls outside.' Nine classrooms originally participated in the study – three classrooms in three different primary schools – although two more were added at a later stage to provide more data on some of the emerging processes. The following introduces the classrooms, their teachers and the schools. Since the study was carried out in Malta, an island state of only 400,000 inhabitants, information is kept to a minimum to protect anonymity. Information that might have compromised anonymity in any way has been left out, even if this meant that the classroom and

1   See Appendix.

school portraits would lack detail and colour. Obviously, all names of schools, teachers and pupils have been changed and figures rounded up.

THE RED ROBIN PRIMARY SCHOOL

Red Robin is a medium-sized primary school with an attendance of about 500, serving a relatively mixed community though with more pupils coming from the higher socio-economic groups. There were about 25 classes ranging from the kindergarten to Year 6 (final primary year) and a staff complement of 40 including the head, assistant heads, class teachers, kindergarten assistants, facilitators, secretary, clerk and caretakers.

One characteristic of the school was the spacious and welcoming environment, with pupils' work exhibited everywhere – the entrance hall and adjoining corridor being virtually a showcase of pupils' work and school initiatives. The head, assistant heads and school secretary were all placed in one office, which was the nerve centre of the school with non-stop visits by pupils, staff, parents and others.

The school had recently embarked on a number of initiatives and projects to make the environment more attractive and comfortable for both pupils and teachers. These included the refurbishment of the administration and reception areas, new furniture for offices and classes, whitewashing corridors and classrooms, the provision of a library and resource centre for teachers and pupils and a new playroom for the younger children, posters for exhibiting pupils' work all over the school and plants in different parts of the school. The school projected its image as a centre of excellence in pupil learning and achievement, high staff commitment and dedication, and parental cooperation and involvement.

Ms Tania's class (Year 3)[2]

This was a Year 3 class with 20 pupils and a relatively young female teacher. It was situated in a cluster of four classes in one wing of the school, with the surrounding landing exhibiting a colourful display of pupils' work. The pupils were seated in groups of three or four, with the library, science table and computers at the

2   Primary school education in Malta is made up of a six-year compulsory programme, starting from Year 1 (six-year-olds) up to Year 6 (11-year-olds), the latter being the last year of the primary cycle. The primary schools are sandwiched between two kindergarten (nursery) years and five years of secondary education. The kindergarten centres and the primary schools are mixed, but boys and girls attend separate schools (state) at the secondary level.

extreme ends of the room. The classroom was practically a showcase of pupils' work. As one went in, one got the impression of a group of well-behaved and highly engaged pupils working within a colourful, friendly and collaborative environment. The researcher's role in this class was that of a participant observer, helping individual pupils during learning activities. A very good relationship was established with the pupils, many of whom sought help with their work. High expectations and interactive, experiential learning activities were two salient features of this group.

Ms Jane's class (Year 4)

Ms Jane worked very closely with the other two Year 4 classes at the school described below. A teacher with long years of experience but also with a creative and innovative approach to teaching and learning, Ms Jane had an open-door classroom and the other teachers in the same landing frequently visited her class. She worked very closely with them. The 20 pupils in the classroom were seated in five groups of four, with the teacher's desk at the front and a facilitator at the back. The pupils with individual education needs and the facilitator were, however, fully involved with the rest of the group. During the observations the researcher sat at the back of the class near the facilitator and took a more passive observer role; during group work he used to go and observe the pupils working. Some of the salient features of this class were collaborative learning, opportunities for self-directed learning, participation in decisions and teamwork with colleagues.

Ms Gertrude's class (Year 4)

This classroom was rather crowded, with 28 pupils sitting in a big horseshoe, and with few charts on the walls. A facilitator sat with her pupil at one end. This class was known for its high expectations, the high level of pupil and teacher enthusiasm and motivation, and meaningful engagement. One of the most striking features was the pupils' and the teacher's pride in their class and their strong sense of classroom belonging. Usually the researcher sat among the pupils and participated as a 'learner' by doing the same activity as the pupils. Pupils were very interested in the researcher, exchanging jokes, telling stories, asking questions and showing work. The high level and quality of pupils' interactions in the activities was remarkable. Ms Gertrude worked very closely with Ms Jane and Ms Pauline.

Ms Pauline's class (Year 4)

This was another Year 4 class and Ms Pauline worked very closely with Ms Jane and Ms Gertrude. Ms Pauline was an experienced teacher who kept herself regularly updated in her professional development by attending seminars and courses, reading, using the internet and exchanging material with colleagues. The class had 26 pupils seated in groups of five or six with Ms Pauline's desk placed next to the whiteboard. This was one of two classes which participated in the study at a later stage, with only a limited number of observations and an interview with Ms Pauline. The most marked feature of the class was the high level of pupils' motivation and engagement, the frequent use of small group work and the emphasis placed on teamwork and collaboration in Ms Pauline's work.

THE BLACKBIRD PRIMARY SCHOOL

Blackbird Primary was a small primary school with an attendance of about 200, serving a relatively socially disadvantaged area. There were 15 classes, with an average of 16 pupils per class and a total staff complement of around 30. The school was well kept, with pupils' work exhibited in the main entrance hall and the corridors. It had among other things a large playing ground and a state-of-the-art complementary teaching room. One got the feeling, however, of being lost in a large, empty and grey building. The school had engaged in a number of initiatives to improve learning, attendance and behaviour, support pupils with learning and psychosocial difficulties, and recruit parents' support and involvement.

Ms Veronica's class (Year 2)

This was the first of two Year 2 classes participating in the study, both classes situated side by side on the same floor. Four groups of three to four pupils (each with an animal's name) were placed around the middle of a spacious classroom. Besides a teacher desk at the front, there was a facilitator desk. The classroom was a showcase of pupils' charts and crafts. The classroom teacher was a young female graduate with a couple of years' experience at this school. Group work, cooperative learning and active learning experiences were the most salient features of the class. The researcher was given an active, participative role in this class, usually helping one of the groups with their work, and establishing a very good rapport with the pupils.

Ms Josephine's class (Year 2)

Ms Josephine's class shared many similarities with the adjacent class of Ms Veronica including size (15 pupils), layout (groups of four) and environment (colourful pupils' work all over the classroom). There was very close collaboration between Ms Josephine and Ms Veronica and they frequently consulted each other during the lessons. Ms Josephine had been teaching for a long time at this school, and her classroom was characterised by her own and her pupils' enthusiasm and engagement, the strong affiliation between herself and the pupils, and the presence of humour during lessons. The researcher's role in this class was more of an observer, sitting at one side of the classroom. A good rapport, however, was established with the pupils, with the researcher quickly learning most of the pupils' names as they frequently came over to show their work, their stars or some activity book.

Ms Maria's class (Year 4)

This was a Year 4 class consisting of 16 pupils, a young but experienced female teacher and a facilitator. Pupils sat in three rows facing the whiteboard, with a small group of four at the front by the teacher's table. The class was divided into groups as well as into pairs. The facilitator sat at another desk at the back. There was a very relaxed atmosphere in this class, with Ms Maria and her pupils being on very friendly terms, and pupils helping each other regularly during work through various peer tutoring schemes. Pupils were consulted in many of the decisions made in the classroom and in setting the classroom behaviour rules. Ms Maria gave priority to the pupils' socio-emotional learning, investing time and energy in supporting the pupils' affective needs. The researcher participated actively in this group, both during the lessons and in supporting pupils during written work.

THE BROWN SPARROW PRIMARY SCHOOL

Brown Sparrow was a large primary school with a pupil attendance of over 500, serving a mixed intake of pupils coming from a variety of socio-economic groups and cultural backgrounds. There were more than 30 classes with an average class size of 20 and a staff complement of 50. The school was spacious, with a large playing ground, a library and resource centre and a large auditorium where school activities were held regularly. The school had taken a number of initiatives to improve pupils' learning and behaviour and to operate as an inclusive community, organising staff development in these areas, recruiting the support of professionals and parents, and participating in national and international projects.

Ms Bernie's class (Year 2)

This was a Year 2 class of 22 pupils sitting round in a horseshoe with four tables in the middle. Ms Bernie was a middle-aged teacher with long years of experience teaching infants. In a prominent side of the classroom there was a religious corner, and after assembly and before lunch Ms Bernie and her pupils used to stand and say a little prayer in the direction of the corner. The nurturing relationship between Ms Bernie and her pupils was one of the clear strengths of the classroom. Learning experiences were frequently experiential, interactive and connected to the children's life and interests. The researcher's role was limited to that of an observer sitting at one side of the classroom and occasionally supporting some pupils in their work, but with frequent contact with pupils who came over to show their work or to say hello. An excellent relationship with the teacher and pupils developed over the weeks.

Ms Lara's class (Year 3)

This was a Year 3 class consisting of 16 pupils sitting in an L shape. Besides a young female graduate teacher, there was also a facilitator sitting next to the teacher's desk and by her pupil. Another pupil with attention and behavioural difficulties was conspicuous most of the time. The classroom was characterised by a diverse, mixed-ability group. The facilitator took a very active role in this class. During his observations, the researcher sat near one of the pupils helping him or her with the work. The most striking feature of this classroom was the excellent teamwork between Ms Lara and the facilitator, with the latter participating very actively in the teaching and learning processes. The researcher did not have many opportunities to observe this group.

Ms Sunta's class (Year 4)

The class consisted of 20 pupils in groups of three or four in a rather restricted space. There was a mixture of abilities, with Ms Sunta frequently engaging in individualised and differentiated teaching, and pupils tutoring one another. Some of the features which stood out in this class were the celebration of diversity, the focus on learning for all pupils and the teacher's positive and high expectations for her pupils. Both Ms Sunta and the pupils were very proud of their group and had a strong sense of classroom belonging. The researcher's role was that of an observer at one side of the class, occasionally helping some pupils with their work.

Ms Erica's class (Year 3)

Ms Erica was a young Year 3 teacher who had been teaching for only a couple of years since her graduation. The class consisted of 18 pupils spread out in groups of three or four; the walls were all covered with pupils' work and there were various tables with their crafts and artwork besides the library and science tables. Ms Erica joined later in the study and her involvement was limited to a couple of observations and a semi-structured interview. The most marked feature of this classroom was the enthusiastic engagement of the pupils, cooperative learning, the focus on including and supporting one another in the classroom activities, and the use of resources connected to the pupils' experiences. Ms Erica sought to promote more autonomy in pupils' learning and in resolving conflicts. She was very eager to put into practice what she had just learned during her initial teacher education course.

CHAPTER 4

Caring Classrooms: Building Connections with Pupils

This chapter, along with Chapters 5–8, provides accounts of good practice in the various aspects of the classroom. It is different from the ground covered so far in being more practice-based. While this chapter focuses on teacher–pupil relationships the next will cover relationships among the pupils themselves.

> We like her because she is always joking with us…explains everything so that we can understand… When I make a mistake she does not shout at me… This is the best teacher we ever had… Even if we are many pupils, the teacher still takes care of us. (James, a pupil in Ms Maria's class)

Teachers today are facing increasing pressure to ensure ever higher levels of pupil performance and passes in examinations. Their own, and their school's, effectiveness are most often measured solely on the basis of academic achievement. This narrow focus on performance has led many teachers, against their better judgement, to reduce the amount of attention they pay to pupils' social and emotional needs and to classroom relationships.

The focus on social processes in education does not, however, weaken achievement, nor is it a distraction from learning. On the contrary, an ethic of caring is at the heart of teaching and learning, providing a foundation upon which effective learning and success can be built and socio-emotional competence developed (Noddings 1992). Caring not only fosters the socio-emotional aspect of pupils' development, it also enhances their intellectual abilities. Pupils who feel trusted and valued internalise the values and goals that the teachers hold for them and are more likely to be motivated, to work hard in the classroom and to engage in those behaviours that are expected of them

(Connell and Wellborn 1991; Wentzel 1997; Werner and Smith 1988). In classrooms where teachers keep all the goals of schooling in mind, pupils achieve more than in classrooms with an exclusive focus on achievement (Caprara *et al.* 2000; Layard 2005; Shann 1996; Willms 2003).

Broadening the educational agenda is not only ideological and philosophical, but is also backed by scientific evidence. Research in neuroscience is challenging many of the earlier claims of brain-based research, re-emphasising the importance of emotional engagement in learning. Stress, fear and anxiety cause the blood flow to move away from the neocortex, the seat of cognitive processes, towards the brain stem. By contrast, a relaxed and positive affect state triggers neurochemical changes conducive to learning (Geake 2006; Geake and Cooper 2003). In other words, learning occurs in a classroom climate where pupils feel physically and psychologically safe. This concurs with what Abraham Maslow proposed around 40 years ago, that higher-level needs such as learning will only occur once the needs for safety and security have been addressed (Maslow 1970).

> When schools focus on what really matters in life, the cognitive ends we now pursue so painfully and artificially will be achieved somewhat more naturally...children will work harder and do things...for people they love and trust. (Noddings 1988, p.32)

Responding to those feelings will lead to a caring relationship, a 'connection or encounter' which satisfies a need shared among all human beings. One of the most important encounters in the classroom is the relationship between the teacher and the pupils. It provides a psychological structure within which individuals can grow and thrive as healthy human beings. A caring teacher–pupil relationship is a highly protective factor for children. It is associated with positive interactions with peers, emotional regulation, academic achievement and fewer behaviour problems (Pianta 1999; Pianta and Sternberg 1992). This protective effect operates for all pupils in the classroom, but appears to be particularly significant for vulnerable children (Pianta 1999). Werner and Smith (1988) found that, among the most frequently encountered positive role models in the lives of resilient children outside the family circle, was a teacher with whom the pupils had built a close relationship and who served as a positive model for personal identification. Teacher care and support have a distinct impact on pupils' engagement, motivation, achievement and socio-emotional wellbeing (Davies 2003; Wentzel 1998).

Box 4.1 Going down memory lane

Going back to our past school days, there is certain to be at least one teacher who had a special place in our school experience, with whom we felt comfortable, safe and valued. Reflect on this experience and on those qualities which that particular teacher exhibited which made us like him or her, and consequently school and learning. We might all have our different reasons, but one likely common theme is a caring relationship where we felt accepted, supported and cared for.

OVERT EXPRESSIONS OF WARMTH AND AFFECTION

Ms Bernie is a Year 2 teacher in a mixed class of seven-year-old pupils. One of the hallmarks of her classroom was the close relationship she had developed with her pupils. It was one of her qualities in her long years of teaching:

> I am not up there and they down here, I am more like a friend, and the kids love me, they give me cards, they tell me, 'Miss I love you very much', or 'How smart you are dressed today, Miss!' I love children and I love teaching children.

This statement resonates with Nias' (1999) assertion that teachers in primary schools tend to see themselves as parents as well as teachers, as young children tend to evoke natural feelings of care and affection in adults. Indeed Ms Bernie expressed her belief that pupils needed to be protected and cared for at school, and she expressed concern when any pupil was upset, hurt or sick. The first thing she did in the morning as the pupils came in from the morning assembly was to say a prayer for pupils who were sick on that day. During the break she spent time listening to the stories and concerns the pupils brought with them during that day, while celebrating birthdays and special occasions was a regular feature of the classroom. She saw the class as filling some of the roles usually falling within the remit of the family, providing a safe base for the pupils:

> The busier the parents get, the more important the school is getting in character formation, and parents themselves have come to rely more and more on the school for their children's development.

Ms Bernie cared for the pupils out of an inherent human interest in the wellbeing and welfare of the children entrusted to her. Her care and support was not conditional upon pupils' achievement or progress. Sergiovanni (1994) calls this 'substantive' caring where caring for pupils is demonstrated as a core value, an end in itself rather than as a tool to get better results. Noddings (1995) defined caring both in terms of caring for somebody else as well as being cared for. The pupils returned the care and affection of Ms Bernie, and they gave her cards and presents on various occasions. One little girl described her relationship with Ms Bernie: 'The teacher takes care of us... We play with her, she makes us happy, we love her and she loves us, she is like our mother.'

This expression of affection for the teacher resonates with similar statements by older pupils in other classrooms. James, a nine-year-old pupil in Ms Maria's class, expressed his liking for Ms Maria, a teacher who put relationships at the heart of the classroom. He expressed his appreciation at the attention, care and support provided by Ms Maria during learning activities (see the quote at the beginning of the chapter). Similarly Amanda, a Year 4 pupil in Ms Sunta's class, was very happy with her teacher's encouragement, care and support:

> One of the things the teacher tells us all the time is to try things out, not to give up. She says, 'If there is a difficult sum, we have to win, not the sum, we must not be afraid, we have to use our brains'...and when it is examination time, she tells us not to be afraid... I had many difficulties in Years 1 and 3 but with this Miss I have made a great improvement.

Pupils become attached to teachers who provide positive experiences for them and who tell them and show them that they care about them. They get close to teachers who talk with them, listen to their concerns, make positive comments about their work, express belief in them and encourage them in their learning.

MAKING EFFORTS TO GET TO KNOW THE PUPILS

The first step in getting connected with the pupils is for the teacher to get to know the pupils while giving them opportunity to know him or her as a person. Making the pupils feel safe and comfortable in the classroom and spending time with them, discussing and sharing experiences and discovering what they like and dislike, and consequently incorporating these into the classroom activities, are some of the initial strategies the teacher may employ in establishing rapport with the pupils. As Ms Maria, a Year 4 teacher, remarked: 'It is very important to get to know the pupils individually at the start of the year...You cannot teach the children unless you know their abilities, needs and interests.' At the beginning of the year she opened an individual portfolio on each pupil in which she included all the data she considered relevant, such as notes on any difficulties the pupils were facing, information from parents, records of achievement and lists of the pupils' strengths and interests. In the beginning the pupils filled a handout THIS IS ME with detailed information on themselves which was also included in the portfolio (see Figure 4.1).

Ms Erica, a Year 4 teacher, made it a point to spend half an hour Circle Time with her group every week, particularly during the first term. The first sessions were dedicated to getting to know each other, so that both she and the pupils could learn more about each other. Activities included:

- sharing one thing about me with the others
- one thing I am good at
- if I were an animal
- one thing which can help me to learn better is...
- one thing about my family
- one thing I would like in the classroom.

Later on, she used Circle Time to discuss issues related to the group's development as the scholastic year progressed and to discuss and resolve classroom issues such as episodes of bullying, helping each other with work or preparing for exams. Ms Erica found that this helped to create a positive climate in the classroom, with pupils being more open and trusting of each other and feeling more secure and happy. She also believed that it enhanced the teaching and learning process, as after the sessions the pupils became more motivated and engaged.

> I think that in the long term the use of Circle Time had a positive effect on the pupils' attitudes towards learning...and it helped me as well, I got to know the pupils more, what they like and do not like, their interests.

An example of how Circle Time may be organised by the classroom teacher is found in Case study 4.2.

SPENDING 'QUALITY SOCIAL TIME' WITH THE PUPILS

Ms Maria made it a point to spend some 'quality social time' with the pupils every day, particularly during the break and when meeting the pupils first thing in the morning. She enquired about how they spent the previous evening, about special family occasions, family or community celebrations, the local football team results or events in the news. The pupils appreciated this opportunity to listen to each other and to be listened to, to share and celebrate their stories and experiences together. They felt good in this group and wanted to be part of such a great group. They knew they had to work, and work hard as the examination was drawing near, but they looked forward to those few minutes when they could

Case study 4.1 Circle Time in the classroom

Circle Time is a collaborative classroom activity where pupils can share their experiences, concerns and ideas in a safe and caring environment. All the pupils are given a chance to be listened to and contribute their ideas and suggestions. Circle Time facilitates dialogue and communication in the classroom, providing the opportunity and the climate for developing and strengthening relationships both among the pupils and between the teacher and the pupils (Mosley 1993, Mosley and Tew 1999). It helps pupils to develop important classroom skills such as effective communication, collaboration, conflict resolution and problem solving. In order to organise a Circle Time session, arrange the class in a circle. Introduce the theme for discussion which may have been raised either by yourself (concern about behaviour, bullying, working together), by the pupils (such as through a question box) or as a result of a classroom incident. Each pupil is invited to speak without interruption (sometimes with the help of an object that is passed around, or else a round robin) but they may 'pass' if they do not want to contribute. Agreed ground rules are observed throughout the session, including confidentiality, one person speaks at a time, everybody's suggestions are welcomed, others are listened to without interruption and sarcastic and negative put-downs are avoided. Do various rounds including a discussion of the nature of the problem and recommendations for actions to be taken. At the end summarise the contents of the session and the suggestions which have been agreed upon by the group, including how these are to be implemented. Place great value on ideas coming from the pupils. Conclude by celebrating the success of the session. Sessions usually last about 30 minutes. More information on Circle Time may be found on:

www.circle-time.co.uk

relax and enjoy themselves together. They also knew that, once social time was over, everybody would get down to work again – there was little need for remind-ers. They were very grateful for Ms Maria's efforts to give them a chance to spend some minutes opening up and getting close to each other. These shared experi-ences helped to connect the group members around common interests and values,

This is me

Fill in this handout by completing the sentences about YOU

I am good at:

I like:

My hobbies are:

I have an interest in:

One subject I am good at is:

One subject I am not so good at is:

I have problems with:

I need help in:

I can help in:

My friends are:

Figure 4.1: A handout from Ms Maria's pupils' portfolio

giving them a collective sense of identity and belonging as a community. As Ms Maria put it:

> On my part I try to create an atmosphere like home, I give priority to respect towards the teacher, but not to the distance between us... I joke with the kids as if they were my brothers and sisters or my cousins... We share aspects of our lives as well... Our motto is that we as a group protect each other.

Ms Maria made it a point to share her likes and interests with the pupils, particularly during break time, but occasionally during instruction time as well. The pupils knew the musical tastes of Ms Maria as well as her passion for the local football team. On Mondays the group spent the first few minutes discussing enthusiastically the result of the weekend games; as the football season reached its climax, the discussions became more animated. It was an excellent icebreaker for the beginning of the week, particularly for those pupils who needed some time to settle down again after the weekend. Occasionally the pupils themselves gave examples during the lessons from this shared experience, such as the name of one of Ms Maria's favourite records.

Case study 4.2 Ms Sunta's return party

The organisation of a surprise party for Ms Sunta, who was returning from a brief absence due to illness, was a manifest expression of the pupils' connectedness to their teacher and to each other. Ms Sunta had been absent for a couple of weeks due to a severe cold. The pupils were concerned and upset and had been praying daily for their teacher to get well and return to school. On Friday they got to know that Ms Sunta was returning the following Monday. Together with their parents and the head of school, they prepared a surprise welcome party. A big cake was laid on the table and each pupil made a 'welcome back' card and these were hung up around the classroom. There was a big celebration in Ms Sunta's class that day, and the whole school and the parents got to know about it as well. As one of the proud pupils put it: 'We never had a good teacher, but now we have one, and she's the best.'

'HUNTING FOR GOLD'

It was the time of the Eurovision Song Contest, an event which created great interest in the local community as the country's representative got one of the best-ever placing in the contest. During the social quality time, as the whole class was talking excitedly about the event, Ms Maria asked Yanica to sing the now famous song to the whole group. Yanica's face shone as the whole group applauded her effort. Ms Maria explained how her relationship with Yanica started on a very difficult note, with the child frequently engaging in oppositional behaviour. Ms Maria, however, took time to patiently build a good rapport with Yanica, to know her strengths and needs. She discovered that Yanica was good at singing and dancing. She encouraged her and her mother to develop this talent and gave her every opportunity to do so at school as well, such as participating in school concerts. By Christmas Yanica's oppositional behaviour had disappeared and she was actively engaged in the classroom activities, despite her learning difficulties.

Robert Pianta (1999) refers to this process as 'banking time', where vulnerable pupils are provided with the opportunity to engage in pleasant and non-stressful interactions, helping connections to get cemented and strengths to emerge. He refers to the high affordance of activities such as story telling and playing games for vulnerable pupils, helping to build the children's resources to overcome the stresses in their lives. Making it possible for the pupils to feel good about themselves and their strengths, even if none may be initially apparent, is a powerful way of establishing a rapport and enlisting their active interest and engagement to make him or her an 'ally'.

EMOTICONS

Ms Erica described how the use of 'emoticons' helped her to get to know the pupils better and encouraged the pupils to express and share their emotions with each other. It started with Mario, a pupil with communication difficulties, who was having difficulty expressing and sharing his feelings and needs to others. One of Mario's strengths was his ability to use the computer. Ms Erica encouraged Mario to download and print emoticons, a set of friendly faces expressing the most common emotions. She made use of stories to explain the different feelings on the emoticon cards and taught Mario to use the different faces to communicate his feelings with her. Mario learned to show Ms Erica the happy face when he was pleased with something he had done, or the sad face when he was feeling upset about his work, or to tell her he was feeling afraid or anxious when there was too much noise in the classroom, or that he was getting nervous or angry when some of his peers were getting too intrusive. Ms Erica introduced the cards to the whole class during Circle Time and, after having a discussion on the feelings expressed

	5	4	3	2	1	0	
Affective My relationships with pupils are quite warm and engaging							*Affective neutrality* My relationships with pupils are like those of a professional to a client
Collective orientation I encourage collaborative learning and support between pupils							*Self-orientation* I encourage an individual orientation on the part of pupils
Particularism I take into account the unique features of a disciplinary incident							*Universalism* I deal with discipline incidents according to predetermined protocols
Ascription I value pupils for being whoever they are, regardless of how well they do							*Achievement* I value pupils for their cooperation and achievement
Diffuseness I believe that you need to know pupils well to teach them well							*Specificity* I believe that I can enact my role well with little tailoring to individuals
Substantive I demonstrate care for pupils as a core value							*Instrumental* I demonstrate care for pupils in order to get better results

Scoring and interpretation:
Scores towards the left column (5) suggest that you perceive your relationships as caring. Scores towards the right column (0) suggest a more rational and performance-related way of construing classroom relationships. Where do you stand? Are scores significantly different on any of the six dimensions? Are there any areas that need to be developed? If yes, how?

Figure 4.2: The caring teachers framework (adapted from Sergiovanni 1994)

by the different faces, she gave a set of the small cards to all the pupils. Each pupil then chose one card that expressed how he was feeling that day and described briefly his or her feeling. This activity was repeated informally on other occasions, such as the first thing in the morning or when the pupils needed a break, or in times of disagreement or conflict. Ms Erica encouraged the pupils to use the cards among themselves during their daily interactions. When pupils appeared upset, sad or angry, she invited them to show her the appropriate emoticon and talk about how they were feeling. This strategy not only helped Mario to communicate better with Ms Erica and his peers, to learn more about himself and to feel happier in the classroom, but it also served to create better relationships both between Ms Erica and the pupils and among the pupils themselves.

CONNECTIVE LANGUAGE

> I am very open with them…and I try to be friends with them and help them behave better… Last year I had three difficult boys…but…the classroom climate helped them, I talked with one of them and I told him, I want us to become good friends because we have to work together. (Ms Maria)

Active listening and empathy are two essential foundation blocks in making positive connections with the pupils. As they feel listened to and understood, pupils become more attached to the person providing such positive experiences in their lives. Ms Erica describes some of the strategies she uses with her Year 4 group:

> I involve the pupils in everything that happens in the classroom… We used to say that children are to be seen but not heard…but I listen to the pupils, it is important to listen to them, and let them express themselves. I do Circle Time in my class and pupils are given time to have their say, to express themselves, it works very well, the pupils love it. When somebody misbehaves, I make it a point to listen to what he or she has to say, and if I am wrong, I admit it, it happened some time ago… When somebody misbehaves, first I try to ignore him or try to use some signal…when he persists then I say, 'Look, we need to talk, finish with your work and then come over to talk.' This is important not to humiliate the pupil in front of the others. So I tell him then, 'Tell me what happened, why did you behave in this way?' I listen to his version without interrupting. Then I tell him my version of what has happened and try to connect his behaviour with previous behaviours, like that he is easily upset when he feels rejected by his peers. Next, we look for creative solutions together, asking him for solutions so that it is his idea, his solution… The pupils appreciate this approach, being listened to and given a say. It is very important to first listen to their view before correcting the pupils.

Pupils' Perception of Teacher Checklist (Cefai 2008)

It is not enough that we think we are caring teachers – we need to ensure that we are perceived as being caring as well. The following checklist will enable you to get valuable feedback on how you are perceived by the pupils and how they see the relationship they have with you. It is to be given to all the pupils in your classroom.

We would like to know how pupils see their classroom teacher. You can tell us more about your relationship with your teacher by completing the following checklist. Put a tick in one of the columns on the right for each of the 12 statements. Make sure you do not write your name.

		Strongly agree	Agree	Disagree	Strongly disagree
1	Our teacher is kind and helpful				
2	Our teacher likes me				
3	Our teacher helps me when I am stuck				
4	Our teacher does not get angry when I make mistakes				
5	Our teacher is very kind when I am sad or worried				
6	Our teacher says nice things about my work				
7	Our teacher listens to my stories				
8	Our teacher is funny and makes us laugh				
9	Our teacher talks with us about our hobbies				
10	Our teacher does the things we really like				
11	Our teacher plays games with us				
12	Our teacher shares his/her hobbies with us				

Scoring and interpretation:
What pattern emerges of the pupils' perception of yourself as a classroom teacher? How caring are you perceived by the pupils? How caring are you come out strongly and in which areas do the pupils suggest that more could be done on your part? To what extent do the pupils' views conform with your own as indicated in Figure 4.2? How can you develop more caring relationships with your pupils on the basis of their feedback?

Figure 4.3: Pupils' perceptions of their classroom teacher

A principal reflects on the change in her discipline to a teaching approach:

> 'I'm looking for solutions rather than just punishments. I'm asking students questions like 'What have you learned from this?' and 'How can you solve this problem?'... Instead of looking for punishment[s], I'm looking to help the child grow. (A head of school, in Dasho, Lewis and Watson 2001, p.99)

Points for Reflection

1. How would you describe your current relationship with the pupils? How caring would you say is such a relationship? Use Figure 4.2 to help you with this activity.

2. How would your pupils describe their relationship with you? How caring and supportive are you perceived by your pupils? Use Figure 4.3 to help you with this activity.

3. On the basis of your assessment, what areas can be considered as your strengths and need to be celebrated and made more use of? And are there any gaps that need to be addressed and developed? If yes, how are you going to develop these areas? Did you find any of the examples listed above by the teachers helpful? Which of these do you think will be most useful to you in seeking to develop better relationships with the pupils?

SUMMARY

- Caring relationships in the classroom are at the heart of teaching and learning; they not only foster the socio-emotional aspect of pupils' development but enhance their intellectual abilities as well.

- Pupils need to feel loved and cared for, to feel connected with their teachers and peers, and to have a sense of belonging to their group.

- A caring teacher–pupil relationship provides a sound basis which helps pupils to grow cognitively and socio-emotionally. It does not weaken academic performance or take away precious time from it. Pupils learn more and achieve more in a culture of care.

- Caring relationships involve making deliberate efforts by the teacher to get to know the pupils and letting the pupils know him or her as a person by spending time and sharing experiences with them, listening to their stories and concerns, giving them a say in what happens in the classroom, encouraging them to develop their strengths and talents, supporting them in their learning and in times of difficulty, and being optimistic and hopeful about improving their learning and behaviour.

FURTHER READING

Alder, N. (2002) 'Interpretations of the meaning of care: creating caring relationships in urban middle school classrooms.' *Urban Education 37*, 2, 241–266.

Bluestein, J. (2000) 'Create a caring classroom.' *Instructor 110*, 2, 35–37. Available at http://content.scholastic.com/browse/article.jsp?id=4428 (accessed 22 November 2007).

Deiro, J.A. (1996) *Teaching with Heart: Making Healthy Connections with Students.* Thousand Oaks, CA: Corwin Press.

Greenberg, P. (2001) 'The comforting classroom.' *Scholastic Early Childhood Today 16*, 3, 47–54.

Houghton, P. (2001) 'Finding allies: sustaining teachers' health and well-being.' *Phi Delta Kappa 82*, 9, 706–712.

Kohn, A. (2005) 'Unconditional teaching.' *Educational Leadership*, 20–24. Available at www.alfiekohn.org/teaching/uncondtchg.htm (accessed 12 December 2007)

Levine, D.A. (2003) *Building Classroom Communities.* Bloomington, IN: National Educational Service.

Mosley, J. (1993) *Turning Your School Around.* Cambridge: LDA (see also www.circle-time.co.uk).

Moss, H. and Wilson, V. (1998) 'Using Circle Time in a primary school.' *Pastoral Care 18*, 1, 27–9.

Noddings, N. (1992) *The Challenge to Schools.* New York: Teachers College Press.

Noddings, N. (2005) 'What does it mean to educate the whole child?' *Educational Leadership 63*, 1, 8–13.

Pianta, R.C. (1999) *Enhancing Relationships between Children and Teachers.* Washington, DC: American Psychological Association.

CHAPTER 5

Prosocial Classrooms: Caring and Supportive Peer Relationships

This chapter discusses peer relationships in the classroom and how such relationships influence pupils' learning and behaviour. It presents various illustrations of pupils helping and supporting each other, and of teachers promoting a culture of support and prosocial behaviour in their classroom by providing opportunities for pupils to know each other, to work with each other, to support each other and to solve conflict constructively. The chapter ends with a reflective activity where you are invited to examine the pupil relationships in the classroom and make suggestions on how these may be improved.

> The most beautiful thing we have in our class is that we are united together, we have each other, we love each other, we agree with each other, and we work and learn from each other…but we are not jealous, I really like that.
> (A group of pupils in Ms Sunta's class)

The above statement by a group of nine-year-old pupils was in response to a question on what they liked most about their classroom. It clearly expresses how significant they found their relationships with each other in their daily classroom life. It is an affirmation that these relationships provided a solid ground on which to build their learning experiences and their socio-emotional competencies. These pupils were very close to sitting for their annual examination upon which they were to be streamed in the following year, yet they gave priority to helping rather than competing with each other. They appeared happy to be with each other, to be part of a 'house of belonging' (Levine 2003) where they felt safe, where they trusted rather than feared each other and where interpersonal relationships were salient features of their contexts. Such a statement may indeed reflect the values that underlined the attitudes and behaviour of this particular group, such as solidarity, sharing and mutual support.

Peer experiences in the classroom constitute an important context for children's and young people's development and behaviour. They produce new demands and opportunities for social and emotional growth as well as academic learning. Various studies have demonstrated that they influence pupils' engagement, motivation, learning and behaviour·at all school levels. Studies which examined peer support and acceptance in the classroom suggested that these factors have a significant influence on pupils' learning and behaviour independent of teachers' behaviour (Connell *et al.* 1995; Wentzel 1998). Pupils who feel accepted and respected by their classroom peers, who have friends with whom they can work, share and play, feel valued members of their group. The consequent sense of classroom belonging is related to positive classroom behaviours like motivation, engagement, performance and positive interactions with peers (Goodenow, 1993; Solomon *et al.* 2000). Newman *et al.*'s (2000) study on the transition from middle to high school, for instance, found that perceived peer support was one of the key factors that made this transition a successful one. Successful pupils reported that they had friends who supported their academic goals. On the other hand, there is clear evidence that pupils who feel rejected by their peers are more likely to disengage from their classroom and school, regarding them as uncaring and disconnecting (Altenbaugh, Engel and Martin 1995; DeRosier, Kupersmidt and Patterson 1994). In a number of studies with young pupils, Asher and his colleagues found that rejected pupils were more likely to be lonely, have fewer and less satisfying friendships, drop out of school and have lower achievement (Parker and Asher 1997; Wentzel and Asher 1995).

> [Classroom] community is a place in which students feel cared about and…care about each other; they experience a sense of being valued and respected…. They have come to think of themselves in the plural…part of an 'us'. (Kohn 1996, p.101)

OPPORTUNITIES TO GET TO KNOW EACH OTHER

One of the key values underpinning Ms Maria's classroom practice is interpersonal relationships. She regularly provides informal and formal opportunities to know the pupils, to let the pupils know her and to get the pupils to know each other. As already mentioned in the previous chapter, the first thing she does in the morning, as the pupils are settling down, is to ask whether anybody has any story or event which happened in his or her family or local community to share with the others. This activity is repeated during the morning break while the pupils are having their lunch. Besides these informal group-sharing sessions, Ms Maria uses other structures and activities to connect pupils together:

- *Pupil of the Day* in the first month of the scholastic year, with an opportunity for each pupil to share his or her likes and strengths with the rest of the class for some minutes; a chart is displayed in the classroom for one week (see Case study 5.2 for a similar activity suggested by Huggins 1997).

- *Small groups* with regular and daily opportunity for pupils to interact with each other and to help each other during work. One classroom rule agreed by the whole group is that if they don't know anything, the first line of support is the pupils not the teacher. The teacher is resorted to only when the pupils in the group are unable to provide the help required.

- *Regular classroom meetings* to discuss issues related to the group, such as to establish classroom rules, how to work together and other issues such as bullying, making friends, self-esteem and being assertive.

Case study 5.1 Sociometrics for harmonious relationships

One technique mentioned by Ms Erica to create more harmonious relationships in the classroom is the use of sociometrics: 'I use sociometrics around the middle of the first term, when the pupils would have started to know each other quite well. It gives you a very good overview of the relationships between the pupils, particularly to see if there are any pupils who are being left out or do not have friends. I try to help lonely children become more accepted and integrated by placing them with peers they like and want to work with. I also use the information on how to make seating arrangements and how to organise the small work groups to make them more productive. For instance, I include in each group a star, a neglected or rejected child, peers who want to work together. I find this formation helps the groups to work better and thus achieve more.'

See Figure 5.2 at the end of the chapter on how to carry out a sociometric test in the classroom.

Case study 5.2 Pupil of the Week

Huggins (1997) describes a simple activity to help build connections among the pupils in the classroom. Each week one of the pupils is selected as the pupil of the week. At the beginning of the week the pupil fills or draws a poster about his or her hobbies and special interests (see below) and puts it on the classroom bulletin board where it will remain on display for the whole week. During the week the class has various opportunities to get to know more about the selected pupil. He or she is also awared special privileges. On Friday, the teacher organises an avtivity called 'A story about the Pupil of the Week' where the pupils write a short story or draw a picture about the special person. Only positive points can be mentioned in the stories. Then the pupil draws a cover for the book to contain the stories about him or her written by his or her peers. The following week the whole procedure will be repeated with a different pupil.

Name: _____

Favourite:

Photograph:

TV show: _____

Person: _____

Animal: _____

Sport: _____

Food: _____

Game: _____

Place: _____

NB. Instead of writing out their 'favourites', pupils could use drawings to illustrate them.

Huggins (1997) suggests another activity, *Classroom Spirit*, to encourage the pupils to feel part of their group. A classroom spirit bulletin board can begin when a positive statement is made about your class – for instance, when a colleague mentions that the class was especially well-behaved during a school assembly activity, the teacher shares the comment with the class, writes it on a card and puts it on the bulletin board. Similarly, when a visitor comments on the attractive art work in the classroom or when a supply teacher expresses appreciation about the pupil' cooperation or hard work, these are reported to the class and put on the board. The pupils are encouraged to read regularly what has been added to the board. This activity will help to increase the sense of belonging among the pupils, promote positive, prosocial behaviours and strengthen the teacher–pulpils relationship.

CREATING A SAFE BASE

Andrew was an active and impulsive seven-year-old boy in Ms Tania's class. His impulsiveness, disorganisation and lack of attention, as well as his learning difficulties, put him at risk of teasing and bullying by some of his peers, particularly by a group of four boys led by Simon. Ms Tania recounts how she took decisive action from the very beginning to stop the teasing and promote more supportive relationships among the pupils:

During a Maths activity when I asked Andrew to come out and work out the answer on the whiteboard, Andrew wrote the wrong answer, and there was some laughter in the classroom. I stopped it, but I let the matter rest at that time. I noticed, however, that Andrew was being teased during other activities as well. I discussed the matter with Andrew who was very hurt about the taunting. This was not a one-off incident. I decided to hold a Circle Time – I got the idea from the PSD teacher who comes for one hour every two weeks – and in a circle we discuss issues such as self-esteem, communication, listening, saying 'no's and so on. I use it when some incident happens in the class, or when I want pupils to learn some new skill, or to celebrate some event together. So with Andrew we discussed the issue of diversity and accepting each other's views and opinions. Together we established a classroom rule that everybody's opinions are valid and that we respect each other's opinions. The rule was written down and displayed by the whiteboard. I referred to it every time it was broken in some way or another. The teasing stopped and I noticed that gradually Andrew became more confident and started to participate more in the lessons. Some other pupils who are usually quiet also started to participate more orally in the classroom.

Creating a safe base helped Andrew and the other pupils to become more confident and take more risks in learning. Circle Time is an excellent strategy to develop classroom relationships and promote more prosocial behaviour. More information on how to make use of Circle Time in the classroom is found in Chapter 4.

PROMOTING A CULTURE OF PEER SUPPORT

> It is a norm in my class that when somebody is finished with his or her work, s/he asks his/her peers if they need any help… This helps them to understand each other and to be considerate of each other in this way they get used to consider the needs of others. (Ms Sunta)

Pupils were considered as a valuable resource for each other's learning in Ms Sunta's class. They were encouraged and expected to help each other, with the class divided in small groups and each group providing support to its members. Supportive behaviours were rewarded and publicly celebrated by Ms Sunta, while fighting or telling on each other was discouraged and often ignored. Ms Sunta herself role-modelled helping individual pupils or small groups, and frequently asked pupils to help each other. Small group work activities were characterised by dialogue, sharing and helping each other, with few instances of telling on others, arguing or conflict. As one pupil in the class put it, 'When there is something I don't know, I ask my friends for help, and when they don't know anything I also help them… I like it when we help each other.'

> We share between us…we help each other to finish work…we play together and do projects together…we help each other to finish early so that we can learn more… We work in all sorts of ways, but we like it most when we work as a team. (A group of pupils in Ms Sunta's class)

Ms Maria started to make regular and frequent use of peer-mediated strategies in her classroom almost by default. Some years ago she had a very diverse group with about five pupils needing individual support during most classroom activities. With limited human resources, she was finding it difficult to support the pupils adequately and one of her colleagues suggested making use of peer tutoring. She had already started a buddy system for a pupil with a physical disability and it was working very well. She introduced a system of work partners, with couples of pupils supporting each other in learning, rearranging the classroom seating so that good pupils were matched with the pupils who needed constant support. Gradually she trained some of the pupils as tutors. Not only did teaching become less demanding and less onerous for Ms Maria, but learning improved, pupils felt better about themselves either as tutors or as supported learners, and the overall classroom climate became more collaborative and prosocial. Case study 5.3 provides a more detailed description of how Ms Maria organised peer tutoring in the classroom.

Case study 5.3 Peer support schemes in Ms Maria's classroom

Work partners

During class work, the class is divided in pairs so that both pupils in each pair can help each other with the work. They consult each other and ask the support of the teacher only when both of them have difficulty. One of the pupils is usually able to work without support while the other would need more support. Ms Maria ensures through regular monitoring that both partners are actually doing their work and that the 'weaker' partner does not rely heavily on the other or just copies from him or her.

Peer tutors

Ms Maria trained a number of pupils as peer tutors to provide support to their peers as requested. She handpicked the pupils carefully to ensure that they were not only good in the subjects they tutor in, but were also among the more mature and popular pupils in the classrooms. She carried out a sociometric test with the whole group to identify the most liked pupils in the classroom, those with whom pupils liked to work and whom they wished to help them in their work. She then provided training through role modelling, teaching one of the tutors herself with the other trainees observing her. She then asked them to tutor one another under her supervision, giving feedback as required and making use of continuous encouragement and praise, gradually leading them to more independent tutoring. She also sought to include pupils who were good in various subjects, including literacy and numeracy as well as computer studies, science, art, crafts and physical education. They also served as tutors during small group work, under her supervision.

Playtime buddies

This is where peer support was first introduced in the class. Tony, one of the pupils in Ms Maria's classroom, needed partial support in going in and out of the classroom because of problems in his motor development. He did not have a learning support assistant since his disability did not impair his movements to a large degree, so it was up to Ms Maria, Tony and the rest of the class, in consultation with Tony's parents, to decide on how best to support Tony in a sensitive way while maximising his dignity and independence. It was agreed during a class meeting that one pupil would help Tony for a whole day including the morning assembly, break times and leaving school. The buddy also had to make sure that during play time Tony was not left alone. If Tony felt that the support provided was not being helpful, he would first discuss it with the buddy and then with Ms Maria. The scheme was voluntary, but all pupils wanted to be Tony's buddies. The scheme worked well. Later on during the year, the scheme was extended to the whole group during play time to ensure that everybody had a play partner/group during play time. Alex, one of the more popular peer tutors in the classroom, took an active role to prevent fighting and quarrelling during play.

PROSOCIAL VALUES THROUGH STORY TELLING

Ms Bernie sought to foster prosocial values through direct and explicit teaching, making use of story telling, religion and other activities to emphasise the need to respect and love one another, to help and share with others, and to forgive others:

> From the beginning, I stress the need of supporting one another, that we are together to work and help each other... We pray for the wellbeing of pupils who are sick on the day and we send them cards, and when pupils have quarrels between themselves, I try to instil in them a sense of forgiveness... I take the opportunity in religion lessons to discuss particular values.

Story telling is one of the favourite activities in Ms Bernie's class and a regular feature in the timetable. The story chosen is usually related to the theme/value of that week according to the scheme of work, but occasionally it may be connected to an incident that might have taken place in the classroom that week:

I do stories on helping one another, forgiving others, making friends, respecting one another, accepting each other, solving conflicts peacefully. I choose appealing books with pictures suited to the pupils' level, but occasionally I download the stories from the internet, invent the stories myself or make use of stories the pupils themselves might have written as part of their class or home work. I use many animal stories as children love animals and relate very easily with them.

Last week we were discussing the value of being kind to one another and not to tell on others or gossip about each other. I did a story about the lonely dog which lost all his friends because some other dogs were spreading false rumours about him. They liked it very much. Usually I read the story aloud to the whole group, showing them the pictures as we go along. Then we have a discussion on the moral of the story, followed by an activity in small groups such as role play, drawing, adding another part to the story. The book is then made available at the little library we have in that corner and pupils may read it during their extra work time. During that week we refer to the moral of the story. Sometimes I refer to it when pupils misbehave or fight with each other. Some weeks ago we did the story of a local mascot, Xummiemu, the Clean Hedgehog, who works very hard to keep his house and the surroundings clean and free of rubbish and whose efforts saved an elderly hedgehog from a serious incident. I made use of this story to encourage the pupils to keep our classroom and our school clean. I referred to it whenever a pupil's behaviour went contrary to that of Xummiemu on the chart.

ENABLING PUPILS TO RESOLVE THEIR OWN CONFLICTS

Providing a structure for constructive conflict resolution is critical for the promotion of cooperative and prosocial behaviour in the classroom. The following excerpts describe how two teachers sought to help the pupils resolve their own conflicts peacefully and constructively.

A win–win road (class) map

Ms Jane recounts how one day a serious fight in the yard threatened to disrupt the harmonious relationships in her group. George, one of the pupils in the class, was fighting repeatedly with a number of his peers during play time. The conflict was creating a cause for concern not only for Ms Jane, but for the whole class and some of the parents as well. After hearing both sides of the story, Ms Jane called a classroom meeting to discuss the issue and try to find a solution. She insisted that the group had to find its own solution to the problem together with her help, but she refused to give or impose a solution herself. The class was divided into small groups with each group coming up with a number of solutions to the problem.

These were then presented to the whole group and examined critically for their effectiveness with the guidance of Ms Jane. In the end the group was able to find a solution, finding the cause of George's behaviour and providing him with the opportunity to participate actively in the group without the need to bully and harass the others. The group appointed also a number of pupils who were to ensure that the agreement was being honoured and to help find a solution should a problem appear again.

The six coloured hats

Ms Erica's classroom was having a relationship difficulty, with two cliques competing with each other both in the classroom and outside:

> I had a problem with some of the pupils at each other's throat and causing a lot of difficulties not only for themselves but for the whole class. There were two small groups of pupils who were continuously competing, fighting and telling on each other. This was evident from the beginning so they must have brought the problem with them. I was becoming worried about the whole situation. I had used the sociometric test which helped a little bit; I changed the seating and the groups, but the fighting continued. I discussed this issue with the peripatetic PSD teacher who used to come to my class every fortnight and she suggested that I try the Six Hats technique by Edward De Bono. We decided to do it together during PSD. First some pupils made six paper hats in different colours as part of their extra work, then we presented the hats and explained the function of each hat. Then we examined the classroom problem step by step, one hat at a time, with each small group writing the feedback on a chart using a coloured marker according to the colour of the hat.

- The White Hat enabled us to examine the facts, namely what was actually happening in the classroom between the two cliques, the arguing and fighting between the two groups.

- The Red Hat then helped us to examine the emotions this problem was causing, the jealousy and anger in the two cliques, the frustration in the other classroom members including myself.

- With the Black Hat we examined the problems this clique fighting was causing us, the time and energy wasted on useless bickering and telling on others, the frequent disruption in the classroom activities.

- The Yellow Hat then presented the other side of the picture, as we made a picture of a harmonious classroom with all of us working together, where we all felt happy and safe, and where the time was spent on learning.

- The Green Hat led to a creative discussion of alternatives which would help to resolve the problem now that we were able to evaluate what was happening in the classroom in a calm and objective way and looking at the issue from different perspectives. We encouraged the pupils to come up with their own solutions on how we can work together peacefully as one group. Various solutions were thrown around and discussed, including changing groups, changing classroom layout and seating, appointing a leader for each clique, involving the parents, other staff and older peers, and training in solving conflicts peacefully.

- The Blue Hat then helped us to conclude on what we had learned together about the problem and what to do about it. It was agreed that the situation had to change as it was creating tension and disrupting the lessons. We agreed to 'disband' the two groups into one whole group, to focus on those things which brought us together as one class, to share and help each other more in learning – I introduced more small group work after this – we also did a PSD session on conflict management and drew a conflict resolution chart, with clear steps on what to do when we are in disagreement. The rules on what to do were written down and displayed in the classroom. It took some time to do it but it is quite simple and it saved a lot of wasted time in the end. I use it sometimes when I have classroom problems which need some in-depth examination before a good solution is found. The pupils enjoy it; they especially like to be involved and giving their own solutions.

Case study 5.4 A shared whole-school vision

The school community at Blackbird's Primary shared a common focus on learning, success for all and prosocial behaviour. One of the key beliefs at the school was that every member should be included in the life of the school, that all pupils were able to learn, and should be supported to do so, each according to his/her own ability. Another salient belief was that all members' behaviour in school should be informed by prosocial values, such as acknowledging and respecting each other's rights and responsibilities, caring for each other, sharing with each other and celebrating diversity. Staff seminars and meetings and whole-school activities and celebrations served as opportunities where these values were promoted and celebrated. Morning assemblies were frequently used to promote prosocial values among pupils and celebrate success; staff meetings and seminars helped to share the common beliefs connecting members together; while whole-school activities such as prize days and publications served to broadcast these common school values. More prizes were awarded for effort, hard work and prosocial behaviour than for academic performance. During the Sports Day, instead of prizes for 'winners', all participants were given a memento for participation. Honouring the achievements of staff and pupils during some of the school activities mentioned above also made it clear to all what practices or attitudes were valued at the school. These rituals and activities were useful tools in promoting a common vision based on prosocial values connecting school members together.

	Complete the following items about the behaviour of your group IN GENERAL. You need to know the pupils well before completing the framework. *Most pupils in this class:*	*Not true*	*Somewhat true*	*Certainly true*
1	Are kind and helpful to each other			
2	Help each other with work			
3	Share possessions with each other			
4	Understand and appreciate the needs of each other			
5	Appreciate and praise the work of each other			
6	Show respect for one another			
7	Like to work with each other			
8	Can work easily in small groups			
9	Work collaboratively without supervision			
10	Seek to be fair in games			

Figure 5.1: A framework for assessing pupils' behaviour in the classroom (developed from Cefai 2004)

11	Include each other in games, activities and tasks			
12	Resolve conflict peacefully			

Scoring and interpretation:
What pattern emerges about the pupils' relationships and behaviour in the classroom?
What are the strengths of this group? What aspects need to be improved? How can such improvement be brought about?

Figure 5.1: A framework for assessing pupils' behaviour in the classroom (developed from Cefai 2004) *continued*

The sociometric test is a simple but useful technique that may be used by the classroom teacher to promote more harmonious classroom relationships and identify and remedy any difficulties in such relationships. It is best used when pupils know each other quite well. The questions asked are determined by the information the teacher needs to collect. Samples of questions may include:

'Who is your best friend?'

'Which pupil would you like to work with in the classroom?'

'Which pupil would you like to play with during the break?'

'Which pupil would you avoid working with if you could?'

In the beginning, it may be advisable to ask one or two questions and to restrict pupil choices to three preferences. Give pupils a piece of paper where they can write the names by the respective questions (you may also use pictures and photos instead of names in classes where pupils may have difficulty writing names). Tell the pupils that there are no right or wrong answers but that true and honest answers are important. Reassure pupils that their responses will be kept in confidence. Include absent pupils as well. Once you have collected all the responses, work out a matrix of all the pupils' preferences and then draw a sociogram which will give a graphic display of the classroom relationships, including the stars of the class, the cliques and pairs, and the isolated, neglected and rejected peers (see website address below for more details on how to do the matrix and the sociogram). Consider the changes you will need to carry out from the analysis of your data, such as helping rejected pupils by putting them in a small group of integrated pupils who did not reject them; organising class or arranging small

Figure 5.2: Sociometric test

groups so that the pupils can work more harmoniously; deciding on best seating arrangements for formal and informal work; and keeping pupils' views in mind when delegating responsibilities. More information on scoring and interpreting the responses of a sociometric test may be found at
www.users.muohio.edu/shermalw/sociometryfiles/socio_introduction.htmlx (accessed on 8 February 2008).

Figure 5.2: Sociometric test *continued*

Points for reflection

1. How would you describe the current pupil relationships in your classroom? How harmonious and supportive are they? Use Figures 5.1 and 5.2 to help you with this activity. The sociometric test in Figure 5.2 will help you to identify pupils who are neglected or rejected, classroom stars who may be useful classroom resources, classroom chains and cliques, and other positive and negative relationship structures in your group.

2. On the basis of your assessment, what areas may be considered as the group's strengths? And which areas need to be improved to enhance more prosocial and collaborative behaviour in the classroom? What changes in classroom arrangement, activities and manage-ment would help to address the targets for improvement? Did you find any of the examples listed above by the teachers helpful? Which of these do you think will be most useful to you in seeking to create ever-more harmonious relationships in your classroom?

SUMMARY

- Peer experiences in the classroom constitute an important context for children's and young people's development and behaviour. They influence their engagement, motivation, learning and social behaviour at all school levels.

- Pupils who feel accepted and respected by their classroom peers feel valued members of their group and engage in positive academic and social behaviours in the classroom. On the other hand, pupils who feel rejected are more likely to disengage themselves from their classroom, regarding it as uncaring and disconnecting, and may be at risk of academic failure and social, emotional and behavioural difficulties.

- The classroom teacher may promote more harmonious and prosocial peer relationships by providing space and opportunity for the pupils to know each other, to share their experiences in a safe environment and to learn together; by discouraging competition and rampant individualism; by creating a culture of mutual support and provide structures and training where pupils can act as tutors for their peers; by promoting prosocial values through story telling, role modelling and reinforcement; and by giving pupils the skills to resolve their own conflicts constructively.

FURTHER READING

Childline (2002) *Setting Up a Peer Support Scheme: Ideas for Teachers and Other Professionals Setting Up and Supporting a Peer Support Scheme.* London: Childline (see www.childline.org.uk).

Cowie, H. and Wallace, P. (2000) *Peer Support in Action.* London: Sage.

De Bono, E. (2000) *Six Thinking Hats,* 2nd rev. edn. London: Penguin Books.

Frankel, F. and Myatt, R. (2003) *Children's Friendship Training.* New York: Brunner-Routledge.

Hawkes, N. (2003) *How to Inspire and Develop Positive Values in Your Classroom.* Cambridge: LDA.

Parker, J.G. and Asher, S.R. (1993) 'Friendships and friendship quality in middle childhood: links with peer group acceptance and feelings of loneliness and social dissatisfaction.' *Developmental Psychology, 29,* 611–621.

Sharpe, P. (2001) *Nurturing Emotional Literacy: A Practical Guide for Teachers, Parents and Those in the Caring Professions.* London: David Fulton Publications.

Sherman, M. (2004) *Sociometrics in the Classroom.* Available at www.users.muohio.edu/shermalw/sociometryfilessocio_introduction.htmlx (accessed 8 February 2008).

Weare, C. (2004) *Developing the Emotionally Literate School.* London: Paul Chapman Educational Publishing.

Wentzel, K.R. and Watkins, D.E. (2002) 'Peer relationships and collaborative learning as contexts for academic enablers.' *School Psychology Review 31,* 366–377.

CHAPTER 6

Engaging Classrooms: Authentic, Inclusive Engagement

Meaningful engagement in classroom activities is a key protective factor in children's cognitive and social development. This chapter presents various illustrations of how the teachers sought to engage the pupils through experiential, authentic activities relevant to the pupils' lives and suited to their levels and interests. In the classrooms the focus was on enjoyable and meaningful learning experiences, away from the dominant focus on performance, examinations and competition. The chapter then describes how the teachers sought to engage all pupils in their classroom, adopting an inclusive pedagogy reaching out to all pupils and providing support as necessary. The chapter ends with a number of reflective activities where you are invited to examine the pupils' engagement in the classroom and make suggestions as to how this might become more authentic, meaningful and inclusive.

When asked about the reasons for their problems at school, pupils who are excluded or who absent themselves regularly from school repeatedly refer to an experience of school that they regarded as irrelevant as one of the factors leading to their disengagement and disaffection. They complain of a curriculum which offers little scope in their actual present lives or their future plans, a pedagogy which leaves them passive and uninvolved, and a system which presents them with no choice but to reject its values in order to protect themselves (Cooper 2006; Cooper et al. 2000; Pomeroy 2000). By contrast, resilient pupils who succeeded at school despite early adverse experiences or difficult social and family backgrounds attribute their success in part to a challenging and engaging curriculum suited to their needs and level (Battistisch *et al.* 1993; Daniels, Cole and Reykebill 1999; Waxman *et al.* 1997a).

Indeed, one of the challenges facing schools and teachers today is how to provide a curriculum with which pupils can engage in a fast-changing world, where the landscape of the new millennium is being defined by developments and issues which were largely absent when traditional curricula were being drawn up. This involves not only making the content of the curriculum relevant to the actual world in which the child or youngster is living, as in the case of the 2007 secondary school curriculum reforms in the UK, but also questioning how connective the pedagogy is. Pupils need to be involved directly in their learning experiences, to ask, reflect, explore and discuss. They need to have tasks suited to their level and interests, to feel included as valued members of the learning community, to be provided with regular opportunities for success and rec-ognition, to enjoy learning. When provided with authentic, experiential and enjoyable learning experiences, they become more interested and motivated, and consequently more engaged in the learning process (Solomon et al. 2000; Wang et al. 199). These experiences satisfy some of the fundamental psychological needs of children and young people, namely the need for competence, success and fun. Clearly classrooms bent on performance and rampant competition with little time for individual support and collaborative learning are very unlikely to provide a climate which satisfies these needs, and are set to leave a number of pupils, particularly the vulnerable ones, frustrated, disengaged and at risk of failure. On the other hand, in engaging classrooms all pupils are provided with:

- experiential and enquiry-based tasks where they can connect learning to their own experiences
- learning tasks suited to their interest, developmental level and pace
- opportunities to experience learning as an enjoyable activity
- opportunities for success and recognition
- support in learning as required
- a focus on learning rather than just achievement
- opportunities to learn together and from each other and to construct learning experiences together
- opportunities to be fully included in the classroom activities.

The following excerpts from the life of classrooms illustrate some of these processes.

ACTIVE AND MEANINGFUL PARTICIPATION

Students engaged in learning make a psychological investment in learning... They take pride not simply in learning the formal indicators of success, but in understanding the material and incorporating it in their lives. (Newman *et al.* 1992, p.12)

Going down memory lane to our old school days, probably the memories most strongly etched in our minds and hearts are those when we were right in the middle of an activity, our hands 'dirty', our classroom messy, all our senses in full action, our excitement infectious. We ourselves were the protagonists of the activity, we felt in control and we were having great fun doing it. It made sense and we learned without effort. Our mind and our heart, our thoughts and our emotions, were connected together in ensuring a long-lasting learning experience. There was no need for rewards or grades to encourage participation. Learning was fun, provoked by 'humanity-reflecting' teachers (Oldfather 1993) and fun-loving pupils. Indeed, the strongest connections in our brains occur when we are emotionally engaged in concrete, meaningful learning experiences (Geake and Cooper 2003).

Soothy the Black Cat

Ms Bernie's classroom served as a friendly learning environment, with instructional arrangements facilitating pupil-centred and activity-based tasks. During an English literature session Ms Bernie introduced the lesson by telling the pupils: 'Today I have a big surprise for you; you have to guess what is in this feely bag.' The bag went round from one excited pupil to another. Finally, the object turned out to be a soft-toy cat and a discussion on pupils' own pets followed. Pupils were then introduced to the world of cats, to the different species, their feeding habits, superstitions related to cats and the usefulness of cats across history. Different pictures of cats were shown. The ensuing poem on *Soothy the Black Cat* thus found all the class excited and waiting in earnest. They sang it together and they tapped its rhythm with their fingers on the tables. Ms Bernie did not mind the sometimes noisy pupils. More fun was to follow as the pupils mimed the story in groups and drew pictures of Soothy as well as their own pets. They shared their drawings and they were encouraged to bring photos of their pets the following week. Ms Bernie's own enthusiasm, use of language matching pupils' development and sense of humour helped to take the whole group through a highly engaging and enjoyable learning experience. As one pupil put it: 'Everybody participates, everybody enjoys it, no one is bored in our class.'

Fun at the beach

During another poetry lesson with a group of nine to ten-year-olds, Ms Gertrude frequently acknowledged pupils' knowledge and skills and made use of their own examples and stories. She asked pupils to write their own experiences on the theme of the poem (*At the Beach*) some days before the lesson. A number of these stories were shared with the whole group, read by the pupils themselves, with Ms Gertrude commenting and elaborating on the stories. The discussion moved from fun at the beach to skin cancer and the protection of the environment. All children could associate the poem with parts of their own lives outside the school, and thus they had their own stories to tell. One part of the activity included the collective construction of a paper aquarium for the classroom, with each pupil contributing a fish, shell, pebble or plant. Ms Gertrude remarked:

> Although I prepare work beforehand, I do a lot of spontaneous teaching and activities according to the situation. I prefer to go with the flow of the children, using spontaneous and creative improvisation...and I take ideas from children themselves because sometimes children teach you themselves.

Cookie the funny parrot

Cookie was the puppet parrot in Ms Josephine's class. He participated actively in the lessons, interacted frequently with the pupils and often expressed his views about what was happening in the classroom. When the classroom needed a laugh, Cookie was always ready with a good joke. He was excellent in defusing tension, raising enthusiasm and creating excitement. During explanations, Cookie sometimes asked questions of Ms Josephine because he could not understand, or asked Ms Josephine not to hurry so that everyone could understand. During class work he asked if anybody needed help. When introducing a new topic or a challenging task, Cookie would sometimes keep on asking questions to ensure all were following and that explanations were repeated if necessary. Sometimes he pretended not to understand, thus 'encouraging' Ms Josephine to use different ways or strategies to explain the topic. When there was an issue between the teacher and the pupils or between the pupils themselves, Cookie always came to the rescue. One day, the pupils did not like the idea of having homework, as they had spent the whole morning on an out-of-school excursion. Ms Josephine was not so sure. Sylvana asked Ms Josephine if Cookie could help with the problem. Cookie jumped up from his place by Ms Josephine's desk, remarking how he had been enjoying his siesta until he was woken up from his pleasant dream. He asked Sylvana what the issue was about. A compromise was reached when one of the pupils suggested just one activity for homework.

Pupils' active participation in decision making such as establishing classroom rules, discussing issues and resolving conflict is discussed in Chapter 8.

AWAY FROM 'THE TYRANNY OF TEST SCORES'[1]

> Politicians and policy makers have reduced the goal of schools and colleges
> to measurable outcomes of a limited sort: *performance* tables, *performance* pay
> and *performance* management. From the confines of their parallel universe,
> they create and disperse lists by which all shall be judged. In order to
> achieve compliance, a sprinkling of fear is added, and under such pressures
> there is that a grave risk that teachers pass this on to pupils. [Yet] the
> evidence is that a focus on *performance* can depress performance: learners
> end up with negative ideas about their competence, they seek help less, use
> fewer strategies, and become organised by the very judgements which do
> them down. And the evidence is that a focus on *learning* can enhance per-
> formance. (Watkins 2003, p.8)

Schools and classrooms are becoming increasingly aware of the risks of succumb-
ing to the pressure to achieve, to measure school success primarily on the number
of pupils who pass annual and entrance examinations. Not only does the achievement overkill become a hazard for children's and young people's personal and
social development, but as Chris Watkins suggests above, it detracts from learning
and achievement as well.

Ms Maria sought to underline her belief in a more humane, personal-social
approach to teaching and learning. Her class was formed of a group of
heterogeneous learners with different educational needs, learning styles and
readiness levels, together with a considerable number of pupils with personal,
family or learning difficulties. All pupils worked hard, but each according to his
or her pace, readiness and style. Everybody could learn and was provided with
the opportunity and support to do so, and everybody made sure that everybody
else was learning. Pupils in difficulty were not seen as keeping the others behind
but as providing an opportunity to offer assistance. Even if the pupils were facing
examinations at the end of the year upon which they would be streamed the
following year, the focus in the classroom was on learning, on learning from each
other and on helping each other to learn. There was a common belief among the
classroom members that learning was the key objective for being together, that
everybody will be provided with the opportunity to learn and that pupils could
learn together and from each other. Prosocial and collaborative behaviours were
rewarded, effort rather than performance celebrated, competition discouraged,
individual and group strengths promoted and socio-emotional literacy given

---

1   Elias, Arnold and Steiger Hussey (2003).

prime time on the daily timetable. The peer group itself was the most valuable and important resource.

The pedagogy reflected the diversity of the learners, with various modes of material presentation, resources and work activities. During a mathematics lesson on time, for instance, Ms Maria sought to make use of multisensory techniques, referring to concrete experiences and objects from real life, encouraging pupils to come up with their own examples, writing and displaying all the steps on the whiteboard, and asking pupils to make their own clocks from cardboard paper. As Ms Maria succinctly put it: 'What is important for us is that pupils learn and enjoy coming to school, that their basic needs are addressed; we all agree on this issue and we do our utmost to address it.'

In keeping with this broader agenda of education, Ms Maria paid considerable attention to pupils' socio-affective needs. As mentioned elsewhere in this book, she sought to create a 'place like home' where pupils felt safe and happy and shared a sense of classroom belonging. She spent considerable time in getting to know the pupils individually and building relationships with them, listening to their concerns, discovering their strengths and making them feel an invaluable part of the group. She referred to a number of pupils who had social, emotional and behaviour problems but who were now happy learning in her class. Her technique was very simple but effective. She spent considerable time trying to reach out and connect with the pupils, focusing on their positive qualities, listening to their problems and instilling self-belief until the pupils could not resist the temptation to become friends. In the end they became what Houghton (2001) called her 'allies' in teaching and learning.

> My target is to win them over, then we can work together for the whole year. But I emphasise that they are very important for me, that I care for them as individuals, they are not just numbers in a group; what happens to them in their life is also important for me.

Clearly, for Ms Maria, to be an effective teacher one has also to be a nurturing educator, ensuring a balance between the academic and affective aspects of teaching and learning.

> We respect each pupil as an individual with his or her own needs, whoever he or she is... I think this is one of the important characteristics of this school... For me it is very important that we work all together, everybody, no distinction between good and weak, in fact those who are ready then help those who are still working.

In Ms Bernie's classroom it was possible for all pupils to get recognition for their effort and success. There were no winners and losers, no best and worst, no competition for the top prizes. Recognition was awarded for both individual and group efforts and achievements. When a pupil, a small group or the whole class accomplished something, especially if it might have been an improvement which required considerable effort, Ms Bernie encouraged the sharing and celebration of the success with the rest of the class and occasionally with other classes and the whole school as well. All pupils had their own strengths and skills and they were provided with opportunities to exercise and use these assets while gaining recognition for their accomplishments and improvement. Besides academic skills, these included drama, singing, art, dancing, football, woodwork, computer drawings, story telling and sharing knowledge in one area or another. The classroom was indeed a showcase of pupils' work and artefacts and often the pupils proudly drew the attention of their peers and classroom visitors to their drawings, cards and crafts. The following comment by a pupil illustrates this mutual sense of satisfaction:

> We did an exhibition together…and we went to show it to the Head and she was pleased with us, and we congratulated each other, and I was also happy that the others did something nice as well.

Indeed in Ms Bernie's class all pupils were entitled to their hour of fame on one occasion or another. One common activity in the classroom was for pupils to bring to school something they may have created or written, such as computer artwork, drawings or crafts, a story or poem, or photos of a family event, and share it with the rest of the class. This might be presented as a brief activity just before or during the break, or sometimes integrated with a lesson as an introduction, such as when Jeanne made a small presentation on dinosaurs, bringing her own collection in during a science lesson. Silvio was a quiet, well-behaved boy with clear difficulties in academic learning. He was regularly supported by Ms Bernie, although occasionally there were indications that he was becoming more aware of his difficulties and this was having a negative impact on his self-esteem. Silvio's father was an amateur statue maker and had a collection of Holy Friday statuettes which he exhibited publicly every year. He had helped Silvio to make his own set of mini statues, and once Ms Bernie got to know of them, she invited Silvio to bring the statues to the class and talk about how he and his father did them together. After the talk, Silvio became the classroom 'expert' on statue making, and some of his peers asked his help to make their own set of statuettes as well.

> Everybody is good in this class not only me… Everybody has something special…pupils who finish work quickly, others who have many friends.
> (Paul, a pupil in Ms Gertrude's class)

ENGAGEMENT FOR ALL

> ...from an educational point of view the core of inclusive education is edu-
> cational engagement...[the] active and constructive social and academic
> involvement in the educational process. (Cooper 2006, p.62)

Reaching out to all the learners

One of the key tasks of the resilience-enhancing classroom is to break down
barriers to ensure that all members are actively engaged in the learning process
and have an equal opportunity to learn and succeed. Placement in a physically
accessible mainstream classroom does not in itself necessarily lead to engagement. The pupil may be physically present with the others but not necessarily
engaged in the learning process. It is the level of meaningful participation by each
pupil that should be the measure of how much the classroom is including that
individual (Bartolo *et al.* 2007; Cooper 2006). In practical terms this means that
the classroom teacher needs to adopt a flexible method of teaching, adapting his
or her approach according to the needs, interests, styles and experiences of the
learners.

Ms Jane was preparing a lesson on environmental awareness which was part
of an EU Comenius project with five other countries in Europe: namely, Spain,
Italy, Austria, Slovenia and Hungary. As an introduction, the pupils brought with
them and presented pictures of the five countries, including flags, maps, posters of
tourist attractions and pictures of locals in traditional costumes. Some of the
pupils who had visited one of these countries told stories related to their holidays.
Ms Jane also showed a couple of brief DVD clips on two of these countries. The
first lesson centred on the various climates. Ms Jane sought to help the pupils
understand the topic by connecting it with the local climate and the different
seasons, and pupils' own experiences of the seasons. As part of the activity, small
groups made use of the classroom computers to draw pictures of the climate in the
various countries. Two pupils who needed help in written work were supported
by Ms Jane and peer tutors. It was a lesson that reached out to all the pupils,
appealing to various learning styles and preferences and addressing the different
learning capabilities of the pupils, including the ones experiencing learning
difficulties.

> Every student is entitled to the promise of a teacher's enthusiasm, time and
> energy... It is unacceptable for any teacher to respond to any...children...
> as though the[y] were inappropriate, inconvenient, beyond hope.
> (Tomlinson 1999, p.21)

Case study 6.1 There are no losers, everybody wins

Ms Josephine explained that there is no competition in her classroom. 'We are a Year 2 class and thank God we do not have tests and exams... I know of some schools which do tests even in Year 1 and send reports to parents with grades...and the pressure is already starting then, with the good pupils and the weak pupils... I do not think this is good education...particularly at such a young age... If you look around here you can see there are no charts with points or stars for achievement...most of the charts and posters have been made by the pupils. If you look at those posters they did about themselves, they show the talents and interests of each pupil. That chart on the animal farm was made by all pupils – Jeremy who is very good in drawing made the farm while the sheep, cows, chicken, goats, pigs, horse, dog, cats, the farm tools, the farmer and his wife, these were made by the pupils, so each pupil has contributed to this farm. I also do a lot of group work in the classroom where pupils work together and help each other; as you can see they are seated in groups of four and there are no front and back pupils, I try to involve everyone. Tony, for instance, is a more practical type and does not like to sit down for long, but he is wonderful with classroom chores; he is also the classroom postman bringing and taking messages to other classrooms and the Head's office.'

Giving all a chance to succeed

Ms Sunta's class consisted of a range of readiness levels, interests and learning preferences. One of the core values she sought to instil from the very beginning was that success was open to all and that the members of the group were going to help each other succeed. She made a point of including all pupils during explanations, practical activities and written tasks. Comments such as 'Always the same hands, we need to see new ones!' and 'I am not sure everybody has understood!' were frequently heard in the classroom. During explanations and class work, she paid particular attention to a couple of pupils who needed more individual explanations.

Peer tutoring was a common practice in the classroom, and pupils had a 'yellow book' list of trained tutors who could help, depending on the subject. Ms Sunta also worked closely with the support teacher and the parents of three pupils who had considerable reading and spelling difficulties. She developed individual programmes in reading and writing skills for the three pupils, including special handouts and material. Every week the peripatetic teacher for the deaf visited the class to provide support to Marcella, and again Ms Sunta and the peripatetic teacher discussed the girl's progress and academic programme for the ensuing week. Mario who was seated next to Marcella was also responsible for giving her support during explanations and work.

As the bell rang for the break at the end of a very busy morning session, Ms Sunta gave a sigh of relief. Although looking forward to the break, she sat down and expressed her satisfaction that the kaleidoscope of abilities and learning styles seemed to fit harmoniously all together, in one community of learners. Everybody could learn and everybody helped everybody else to learn.

> The goal for each student needs to be maximum growth from his current 'learning position'; the goal of the teacher needs to be understanding more about that learning position so that learning matches the learner's needs. (Tomlinson 2001, p.15)

'Rescuing' pupils with behavioural difficulties

Pupils with behavioural problems constitute one of the major challenges for teachers working in inclusive contexts. Indeed, of all the categories of individual educational needs, this group of pupils is most at risk of exclusion, with schools having a right to bar such pupils from school (Cooper 2006). Ms Maria saw one of her roles as a 'therapeutic agent' supporting pupils 'in need of rescue' from various social, emotional and behavioural difficulties (Calderwood 2000). Before she started teaching the present group, she had been warned that she had a small number of pupils known for their oppositional behaviour. She was not unduly anxious at the situation, however. From the very beginning she tried to build a caring relationship with them, finding their strengths and giving them roles and responsibilities, while keeping them engaged in the classroom activities and rewarding their participation and effort.

> I have been given some of the worst cases at the school, boys who are very difficult and challenging. However, from the very start I show them that I am not interested in what happened last year, this was going to be a fresh start, they had a chance to succeed. Everybody has a chance and a place in my classroom, whatever his or her ability or behaviour. The important thing is to show them that you care for them and you are interested in them, and that they all have a chance to learn.

This resonates with what Ms Sunta said:

> I don't like the practice of consulting last year's teacher to identify potential troublemakers… I believe you should give each pupil a fair chance without being prejudiced…for instance one pupil who was bullying others last year is really doing well this year, and it was good I did not know about his behaviour.

Case study 6.2 Welcoming John

John was a new pupil in Ms Sunta's class, having just arrived from another country. He did not speak any of the two languages used at the school, but he could understand some English. The first thing in the morning, all the pupils introduced themselves one by one, saying something about themselves, their interests and hobbies. John followed suit through pictures and the teacher's help. In the next round, each pupil suggested one thing he or she was ready to do to help John feel at home and become part of their group. With the teacher's help, John mentioned that he was good in maths and computers; some of the pupils immediately invited John, to join them on the computer during the break. At the end of the session, Ms Sunta told John: 'Everyone is going to help you, John, and if you need anything you may ask me as well!' Later on during the lesson, the teacher publicly praised John's work, and John, who appeared somewhat shy and quiet in the morning, was already interacting with some of his peers during the break. Pupils were asking him one question after the other about his country, his likes and hobbies, and to be their friend.

Points for reflection

1. How would you describe the pupils' engagement in your classroom? How meaningful and authentic is it? To what extent is learning an experiential, authentic and enjoyable enterprise for the pupils? Use Figures 6.1 and 6.2 to evaluate pupils' view on learning.

2. How inclusive is pupil engagement in the classroom? Do all the pupils have the opportunity for meaningful engagement in the

learning process? What adaptations do you make (in content, methodology, resources, pupil products) to ensure that all the pupils have equal access to the learning experiences? Figure 6.2 provides a guide to getting to know the pupils better.

3. On the basis of your assessment, what goals would you like to set in your classroom to improve your current practice? How can these goals be achieved? Did you find any of the examples listed above by the teachers helpful? Which of these do you think will be most useful to you in seeking to facilitate more meaningful and inclusive engagement for all your pupils?

A framework for assessing pupils' orientation to learning (Watkins 2003)				
How do pupils view their learning experiences in your classroom? How meaningful are such experiences for the pupils? Are they focused on performance or do they have a learning orientation? The following questionnaire will assist you in examining the pupils' views on the learning process.				
	We are interested in your views about learning. There are not any 'right' or 'wrong' answers. Can you tell us how you approach your learning? Just put a tick in one of the columns on the right for each of the 12 items.	*Strongly agree*	*Agree*	*Disagree*	*Strongly disagree*
1	I like school work that I'll learn from, even if I make a lot of mistakes				
2	I'd feel really good if I were the only one who could answer questions in class				
3	An important reason why I do my school work is because I like to learn new things				

Figure 6.1: Pupils' perceptions of their learning

4	It's very important to me that I don't look stupid in class				
5	I like school work best when it really makes me think				
6	It's important that other pupils in my class think I'm good at my work				
7	An important reason why I do my work in school is because I want to get better at it				
8	An important reason why I do my work in school is so that I don't embarrass myself				
9	I do my school work because I'm interested in it				
10	I want to do better than other pupils in my class				
11	An important reason why I do my school work is because I enjoy it				
12	The reason I do my work is so others won't think I'm dumb				

Scoring and interpretation:
What pattern emerges about pupils' learning orientation in your class? What are the strengths of this group? What aspects need to be improved? What changes do you need to make to bring about such an improvement?

Figure 6.1: Pupils' perceptions of their learning *continued*

Samples of questions to use (Bartolo et *al.* 2007)

SENTENCE COMPLETION

I am good at _____

I am bad at _____

I like _____

I dislike _____

My favourite hobby is _____

My most treasured possession is _____

I learn best when _____

I often get stuck in my work when _____

YES/NO QUESTIONS

I understand most quickly when things are explained with pictures
☐ Yes   ☐ No

I like to work by myself   ☐ Yes   ☐ No

I like to work in pairs or in groups   ☐ Yes   ☐ No

I like to complete all my work   ☐ Yes   ☐ No

I find it hard to start work   ☐ Yes   ☐ No

I prefer to work fast   ☐ Yes   ☐ No

I like to work on the floor   ☐ Yes   ☐ No

TICKING A LIST

Which topics do you like best? ☐ English ☐ Maths ☐ Science ☐ PE

How do you like to work?   ☐ alone   ☐ in pairs   ☐ in small groups

Figure 6.2: Getting to know the pupils

How do you like to present your work?

☐ verbally   ☐ through drawings/chart   ☐ on tape recordings/CDs

☐ written by hand   ☐ written on the computer

NARRATIVES

Write a story on the best person in your life.

Describe the animal you like best and why you like it.

Describe the best day in your life/your best school day.

Figure 6.2: Getting to know the pupils *continued*

SUMMARY

- A crucial task in resilience building is to secure the active engagement of all pupils in the activities taking place in the classroom.

- Pupils are more likely to become actively engaged in the learning process when they are provided with opportunities to participate in meaningful, relevant, learning-centred and enjoyable activities suited to their interests, experiences and learning styles and preferences.

- A focus on learning rather than on achievement enhances performance. Not only does the achievement overkill become a hazard for children's and young people's personal and social development but it detracts from learning and achievement as well.

- Meaningful engagement satisfies pupils' basic needs for competence, success and fun.

- All pupils need to be meaningfully engaged in the classroom and have full access to the learning process by being provided with tasks suited to their needs, level and style.

- Pupils who need support in their learning will be provided with such support in the classroom through a variety of human and physical resources, a flexible curriculum and a suitable pedagogy.

FURTHER READING

Amrein, A.L. and Berliner, D.C. (2003) 'The effects of high-stakes testing on student motivation and learning.' *Educational Leadership 60*, 5, 32–38.

Bartolo, P., Janik, I., Janikova,V., Hofsass, T. *et al.* (2007) *Responding to Student Diversity: Teacher's Handbook.* Malta: University of Malta.

Burgess, R. (2000) *Laughing Lessons: 149 2/3 Ways to Make Teaching and Learning Fun.* Minneapolis, MN: Free Spirit.

Cooper, P. (2006) *Promoting Positive Pupil Engagement: Educating Pupils with Social, Emotional and Behaviour Difficulties.* Malta: Miller Publications.

Fredrickson, N. (1994) 'School Inclusion Survey (SIS).' In N. Fredrickson and B. Graham (eds) *Social Skills and Emotional Intelligence.* Berkshire: NFER-NELSON.

Gagnon, G.W. and Collay, M. (2001) *Designing for Learning: Six Elements in Constructivist Classrooms.* Thousand Oaks, CA: Corwin Press.

Kohn, A. (2001) 'Fighting the tests: a practical guide to rescuing our schools.' *Phi Delta Kappa*, January. Available at www.alfiekohn.org/teaching/ftt.htm (accessed 22 November 2007).

UNESCO (2005) *Guidelines for Inclusion: Ensuring Success to Education for All.* Available at www.unesdoc.unesco.org/images/0014/001402/140224e.pdf (accessed 8 February 2008).

Watkins, C. (2003) *Learning: A Sense-Maker Guide.* London: Association of Teachers and Lecturers.

Watkins, C., Carnell, E., Lodge, C., Wagner, P. and Whalley, C. (2002) *Effective Learning.* London: Institute of Education School Improvement Network.

Weimar, K. (2002) *Learner Centered Teaching: Five Key Changes to Practice.* San Francisco: Jossey-Bass.

CHAPTER 7

Collaborative Classrooms: Learning and Working Together

This chapter builds on the previous ones, examining classroom engagement within the context of collaborative relationships among pupils. It argues that cooperative learning is more beneficial to pupils' learning and socio-emotional competence than the dominant competitive and individualistic approaches, and presents portraits of pupils working and building knowledge together. The second part examines various episodes of teachers building practice together, sharing practice and planning and teaching collaboratively. The final section discusses the collaboration between the class teacher and the parents, and illustrates how parents may be active and collaborative partners in the academic and social life of the classroom. The chapter ends with a number of reflective activities where you are invited to examine the classroom's interactions and relationships and make suggestions on how these may become more collaborative.

In May 1565 two great armies stood face to face, ready for the greatest siege the Mediterranean island had ever experienced in its thousand years of colonisation. The Knights of Malta had mobilised their forces down to the last warrior, summoning every knight from across the eight languages spread over the European continent. All local men over 18 years were called for battle. Around 8000 knights, soldiers, slaves and local inhabitants stood ready at the bastions overlooking the Grand Harbour as the Ottoman fleet of 193 vessels and 30,000 fighting men sailed into the southern harbour. The two mortal enemies were ready for one final battle. The Knights were determined to stop the Muslim conquest at the southernmost tip of the old continent and to start rolling the expanding Ottoman Empire back to Asia. The Ottomans wanted to destroy once and for all their oldest enemy – the Christian pirates of the central Mediterranean who were continually harassing and looting their galleys. After a siege lasting more than three months in stifling heat, the Ottomans admitted defeat and withdrew, leaving behind more than 25,000 of their soldiers dead. The Grand Master breathed a sigh of relief as his weary, bloodshot eyes surveyed the levelled towns and the dead bodies all around him. He had won the greatest battle of his life and inflicted the biggest defeat till then on the Ottoman Empire, but he had lost a third of his knights and a third of the Maltese population, while the land lay waste and burnt, the towns and villages in ruins.

After presenting the story of the Great Siege of Malta through a multimedia presentation, Ms Erica divided the group in two, the Knights and the Turks. Each group had to draw up a 'charter of wishes', writing down what they wished from the other partner so as to prevent the siege from taking place. They had to agree on the three most important wishes, which they were then to present to the other group. The two groups then discussed and negotiated with each other how they could accommodate the other's wishes. Each group had to explain how the wish would benefit not only itself but the other party as well. Two wishes were common to both from the start: not to attack each other and not to attack each other's galleys. The third common wish was more difficult to find, but finally they agreed upon an exchange of slaves working on the galleys. Ms Erica made use of this 'revisionist' history lesson to underline the benefits of understanding and cooperating with one another, and how collaboration stands to benefit both parties. Both the Turks and the Knights now felt safer at home as well as on the sea where most of their business lay, and they could now concentrate their resources and energy in improving their sea trade and bringing more wealth to their own country. It was also possible that, as their fears and distrust of each other decreased, they might start to work together and engage in joint ventures which they might not have been able to do on their own.

BUILDING KNOWLEDGE TOGETHER

> 'Learning as building knowledge together' draws our attention to the processes through which learners act as partners, communicate in relation to their activity, involve themselves in dialogue, and create a joint product which is more than the sum of the parts. (Watkins 2003, p.14)

Collaboration may not occur naturally in those classrooms where the dominant approach to teaching and learning is that of individual achievement and competition, and where the most important value is to prove oneself, usually at the expense of the rest. In such a culture it is very unusual to see any practical value in working together and spending time contributing to collective tasks. These are likely to be seen not only as a waste of time, but also as a give-away to one's competitor, detracting from one's own advancement and achievement.

There is, however, strong evidence from various fields such as business and education that has consistently underlined the benefits of people working together. For the past two decades eminent researchers such as David and Roger Johnson and Robert Slavin have repeatedly argued that cooperation is superior to both competitive and individualistic approaches in cognitive and social outcomes. In their reviews of hundreds of studies on cooperative learning they have reported that cooperation produces higher achievement rates and promotes more positive relationships and social support between teacher and pupils and among pupils, when compared to the other two instructional approaches (Johnson *et al.* 2000; Slavin 1991). There were more episodes of helping behaviours, greater satisfaction with working in groups and greater interpersonal attraction to other group members. Pupils felt they were more popular, accepted and supported by their peers than when working in individualistic or competitive contexts. When they worked together, they perceived that they could achieve their personal goals more easily if all members of their group also achieved their goals; thus they tended to seek outcomes that were beneficial to themselves and to the other members of their group. Moreover, the more they cared about each other, the more committed they were and the harder they tried to achieve mutual learning goals.

> Where individual performance, certificates, prizes are the currency of self-worth, pupils' attention is diverted from the needs and feelings of others, the very gist of social and ethical development. (Lewis, Schaps and Watson 1999, p.525)

Ms Veronica's class was divided into five small groups with animal names. The layout of the classroom, with small clusters of groups sitting together, emphasised the importance of communication and collaboration. Pupils were able, both physically through the arrangement of the furniture, and by permission from Ms Veronica, to move around and talk and discuss together during activities. They were frequently seen helping each other with the work, consulting and discussing with each other. Ms Veronica made frequent use of group work, and every day there was at least one or more group-based activity. During such activities, recognition was awarded for group effort. The groups were heterogeneous in terms of readiness, interests and ways of learning, but sometimes they were restructured according to the task at hand:

> ...it depends on the task, sometimes it is good the pupils help and learn from each other...sometimes I prefer to group them according to ability

depending on the task... They also need to have different learning experiences and that the weaker ones are not always at the receiving end; they need to work in a group where they can also contribute, so it depends, you have to be flexible. Pupils need a lot of guidance in the beginning, you have to avoid one pupil dominating the group, the groups have to genuinely work together cooperatively. Pupils can learn so much by sharing with each other. (Ms Veronica)

I like to work in groups because it is like you are building something, one knows something, another something else...and also because in a group you share and help others and you feel happy helping and doing group work. (Albert, a pupil in Ms Gertrude's class)

Ms Veronica started the activity by telling the pupils that they were going to make up a story together about a day in the countryside. In groups of three, they were given a handout with pictures and they had to write a sentence together and then come out and read it to the whole group. The story was thus built sentence by sentence from each group. Next, the teacher and pupils wrote the story together on the whiteboard, with Ms Veronica making use of and developing the pupils' contributions. The draft of the story was then put on the board with the groups adding to it or making other modifications. Once the story was finalised, one pupil from each group drew a small picture of each action on the board. Another written exercise in small groups followed, where pupils had to answer a number of questions about the story, with Ms Veronica going round to support the groups in their task. The pupils discussed together and collaborated in a warm climate of enthusiasm, fun and mutual support. Johnson and Johnson's (1991) seminal finding that pupil sharing and collaboration has been found to increase pupil interest, curiosity and engagement in their work, as well as their sense of competence and efficacy, was very evident during this activity.

Collaborative peer tutoring is discussed in Chapter 5.

Case study 7.1 Dudu, the collaborative centipede

During a crafts lesson, Ms Josephine gave the pupils a half-empty milk carton and told them that they were going to do Dudu, a centipede, together. This was going to be a class Dudu and so everybody had to contribute a small part. Without this it would be incomplete. Like Dudu's many feet, they all had to work together so that Dudu could move smoothly and gracefully around. Each pupil first had to draw one part of the body and two legs, colour it, and then join his or her group and compose a larger part of the body. The head was allocated to one group. In the second part of the activity, the five groups joined the various parts together with Ms Josephine's help and Dudu came to life. The pupils were very excited, listening and explaining to each other, asking questions, helping and sharing, waiting patiently, appreciating each other's work. They needed no encouragement or rewards to work together. This was the class Dudu, their own Dudu. Ms Josephine stayed in the background, intervening only to ensure all the pupils were participating, to help pupils or groups who needed guidance, to celebrate with the pupils in their creations and to ensure collaboration during small and whole group work. Indeed, collaborative learning is not only about pupils working together but doing so in a helpful and collaborative way. When one pupil told another in a different group that her group had already finished its part of Dudu, another pupil replied 'We are not competing here!' and Ms Josephine immediately remarked 'That's right! What is important is each group does its work together properly and not who finishes first!'

BUILDING PRACTICE TOGETHER

The school's philosophy is to ensure teamwork so that every member in the team takes full responsibility for the duties that are expected of her/him. Collegiality is ensured as all contribute and participate in the learning process going on at the school. All the staff…firmly believe…[that] together we must aim to…work together as one team, irrespective of status…each and every one of us is responsible and accountable…to maintain and develop collaborative working practices. (From the mission statement of Brown Sparrow Primary)

Collaborative partners and mentors

Ms Gertrude underlined that collaboration is not just between pupils but between all classroom members, including the classroom teacher. Teachers too are learners and they learn all the time from their experience with the pupils:

I have been teaching for many, many years but I find that I am learning and changing my methods all the time. I prepare well beforehand and have a good plan on what to do, but I change a lot according to the flow of the pupils; they have a lot of ideas, and I use their own ideas and material during the lessons. I ask them to write essays and find material which they then bring and present to the whole group as part of the lesson. You need to change according to the group you have... This is really a good group this year, they give you a lot and I adjust accordingly – you have to be spontaneous.

Ms Gertrude also referred to the excellent collaboration between herself and the other two teachers in the same year group. The classrooms had an 'open door', with the teachers frequently seeking and providing support to each other, planning their schemes of work together and sharing resources. While the teachers appreciated their autonomy and privacy, they underlined the benefits of 'being together' and 'opening their doors' to each other. They developed a close collegial relationship, with a deepening sense of synchronicity and mutuality, sharing a collective responsibility for pupils' learning. Ms Gertrude underlined the value she and her colleagues placed on collaboration and her belief that they could be more effective if they worked as a team:

> We are very united as a staff. I really liked to work with my colleagues this year... Even when I am at home preparing, I phone them and tell them, look we are going to do this next week, let us meet... Working with the other teachers was one of my best years, working together as a team sharing and exchanging material...we keep close contact with each other all the time...we adjust the lessons together to make sure we work in unison... We fit like a jigsaw puzzle in our work...it worked out really well for both of us and for the pupils.

Ms Pauline, Ms Gertrude's colleague, remarked that the teamwork was not only beneficial for the staff but for the pupils as well:

> The teamwork between us staff had a strong impact on our pupils because they worked and cooperated together, were not involved in fighting, and took many initiatives... There is high motivation...without undue jealousy and competition, with pupils joining together in groups helping each other...there is good teamwork between the pupils.

The pupils themselves agreed that when their teachers worked together as a team the pupils stood to benefit: 'Everybody [all staff] here agrees together, works together and in this way everybody understands us and helps us more.'

The staff at Ms Gertrude and Ms Pauline's school held a seminar at the end of the scholastic year to review the school's development plan in preparation for the forthcoming year. The presentations and contributions of the various groups, the discussions in the workshops and the developmental process unfolding as the seminar progressed through the day were clear indications that the staff took responsibility to work together towards the achievement of the school's objectives. Groups of teachers were responsible for specific areas and targets, forming part of a greater network striving to reach the school objectives through the contribution of all members. Various members expressed their satisfaction about working and planning their schemes of work together, and remarked that shared responsibility had a positive effect on all of them. The recommendations by the working groups reflected the value they placed on teamwork and the belief that they would be more effective educators as a team. The seminar was an affirmation of collegiality and the building of an identity as collaborative and interdependent colleagues. As one teacher put it:

> Throughout this scholastic year we found the time to consult each other, work together and share and exchange ideas, opinions and good practice…there has been excellent collaboration between us.

'A family of teachers'

The staff at Blackbird Primary were known for their unity and collegiality, an oasis of strength and support in an erstwhile 'failing' school with challenging pupils and difficult parents. The school has now overcome its negative reputation, and the close and supportive relationship among the staff was one of the factors which helped to see the school through the difficult times. During Prize Day, one of the factors mentioned by most speakers as contributing to the success of the school was the sense of collegiality among the staff. The Head remarked how encouraging it was to work in an environment where the staff were so united and working happily together for the pupils' wellbeing, an atmosphere which was having a ripple effect throughout the school. Ms Josephine, one of the older teachers at the school, remarked that that one of the things 'which kept us going was the support and unity among ourselves…teachers here would not ask for a transfer but like to stay here with their colleagues'. Ms Veronica, a newly qualified teacher who had been at the school for a couple of years, agreed that she felt welcomed and supported by her colleagues and that this collegial atmosphere helped her to settle down and be effective in her work:

> We are very close and united as a staff, like another family, a family of teachers… I am very happy here; a collegial, supportive environment which helps you to do your work in the best way possible.

These relationships transcended the narrow boundaries of professional collegiality as the teachers socialised together outside school and cared for one another inside school. The relationship moved 'back and forth' from the professional to the personal, leading to a culture of concern and support for one another. Ms Maria remarked:

Some of us go out together at the weekends, we know each other very well... This helps us a lot in our work because it means that we are working as friends, not competing against each other. We also support each other with problems we may have with pupils; so with the support we give to each other, we understand each other's problems and help each other with them, and as a group we decide who can help whom. I think both ourselves and our pupils are lucky that there is this environment.[1]

A classroom team

Angelo was a boy with communication and learning difficulties in Ms Lara's class and he was supported by Ms Valerie, the learning support assistant. Angelo had both literacy and behavioural difficulties, and Ms Valerie had drawn up an overlapping Individual Educational Programme (IEP) with a number of academic and social targets. The IEP was devised together with Ms Lara and the parents during a transdisciplinary assessment meeting called MAPS. Ms Valerie provided individual support during explanations and written tasks, usually sitting besides Angelo for some time, and facilitated his social interactions during break and social activities through direct and indirect (e.g. Buddy system) strategies. Ms Lara herself frequently interacted with Angelo, asking him questions, helping him with the work or going over to see his progress. She held regular meetings with Ms Valerie to plan Angelo's programme together at least one week ahead. Angelo was Ms Lara's and Ms Valerie's joint responsibility, and they both took an active part in facilitating his learning and social inclusion. Ms Valerie's support, however, was not limited to Angelo, but she helped other pupils as well, depending on the nature of the task at hand. She helped Ms Lara in the preparation of resources such as handouts and ICT programmes and in supporting the pupils during class work. She was regarded as a valuable resource for the whole classroom. In fact it was not always easy to remember that Ms Valerie was originally assigned to the classroom to support Angelo. The excellent collaboration between her and Ms Lara not only benefited Angelo, but Ms Lara herself and the whole class. It served as an excellent role model of collaboration for the pupils.

PARENTS AS COLLABORATIVE PARTNERS

The school pledges to accept parents as partners in the operation of the school, and encourage them to actively participate in decision making. To ensure that decisions are made from a position of knowledge and effective

---

1   See Case study 7.2 Collaborative and supportive administration.

Case study 7.2 Collaborative and supportive administration

Blackbird Primary had a previous reputation for being a difficult and occasionally unsafe school for teachers to work in. One of the key objectives of the school administration team in its effort to bring about change in the school was to create a safe climate where the staff could exercise their roles effectively and rewardingly.

The team began by reaching out to the staff to establish a close relationship with them, keeping this relationship as one of its priorities. Together with the staff, the team devised a plan to improve pupils' motivation, learning and success, reduce misbehaviour, increase attendance and build more cooperative relationships with the parents. Regular staff meetings were held to discuss the plan and reach decisions by consensus to ensure all members owned and were wholly committed to the changes taking place at the school. A full staff complement was ensured, while time and space was made available for staff to meet, plan and share practice together, in some instances the administration supervising the classes themselves. A staff room was opened where staff could meet and work together. A mentoring scheme was introduced so that teachers could support each other in planning, use of resources and behaviour management. For instance, the more experienced teachers supported the less experienced ones with behaviour management and relationships with parents. The newly qualified teachers, on the other hand, acted as a resource on the latest pedagogical strategies. The staff were encouraged to participate actively at the whole-school level, while their extra work in organising concerts, excursions, performances and exhibitions was recognised and compensated in some form or another. For instance, four members of staff who had worked very hard in organising the Carnival concert were treated to a free lunch by the school with some time off as well. During public addresses, such as Prize Day, the administration acknowledged and celebrated the staff's dedication and commitment, underlining how this was one of the keys to the current success at the school. During Prize Day, the teachers themselves were awarded prizes for their hard work and dedication, while their work was exhibited for the visitors and parents.

participation, the school must keep parents informed about what is going on. It is only through collaboration with parents that the school can achieve its objectives. (From the Staff Development Plan of Red Robin Primary)

'A direct hotline'

Teachers are regarded as experts in learning. Parents, on the other hand, are regarded as those who know their children best, and consequently they have an important role to play in the children's education at school. Schools are becoming increasingly aware of the well-documented and positive impact of parents' involvement in pupils' learning and behaviour, while parents are becoming more aware of their right to be active partners in decisions concerning their children's education, and their involvement in education is becoming more visible and more meaningful. It goes beyond the traditional, disempowered exchange of information. Ms Erica describes the 'direct hotline' she has established between the classroom and the parents:

> We no longer meet parents once or twice a year on Parents' Day. I meet the parents at the beginning of the year to establish a basis for regular exchanges through the year. I send them monthly reports and we have termly Parents' Days. I introduce the communication book in the first meeting – it is a very good link – and with the internet it is even easier to keep regular contact with some of the parents; some prefer an email to the communication book. The communication book is a direct hotline between us and the parents; we write in it anything which is helpful for me or the parents. The parents write mostly about homework, particularly when their children are having difficulties with it; this gives me good information about the topics some of the pupils are still grappling with. Sometimes they make suggestions such as less or more homework. They also ask me about the supplementary books they can buy to reinforce what I am doing at school…some parents want to know what we will be doing next so that they can prepare their children for the coming topics. We also communicate on pupil behaviour but I try to avoid using the communication book as a report book; I try to report more positive comments than negative ones, like when they did something really well or there was an improvement in behaviour. Sometimes we also make appointments through the communication book.
>
> When I have pupils with learning or behaviour difficulties I keep regular contact with the parents to see how we can help their children. When we hold meetings at the school to plan an IEP for a particular pupil, the parents are invited to come and attend the session and they contribute to the IEP goals. Some weeks ago Victor was giving me trouble in completing work, his work was getting sloppy, he was answering back, etc. When it went on, I sent a note to his mother and we met to discuss the issue. It

turned out that Victor was having some problems at home as well and he was feeling neglected. I dedicated more time for him, giving him more attention and encouragement; his mother also helped as she rewarded his efforts in the classroom. I also offered to go and visit her at home after school hours if need be; sometimes parents cannot come to school as they are working. Together we helped to put Victor back on track.

It is crucial to have parents on your side. For instance some years ago there was a small group of parents in this school who were creating problems for the whole school, shouting in the corridors and classroom. With the help of the administration, the abusive behaviour was stopped and they were not allowed to threaten the teachers in the classroom. At the same time though the staff listened to their concerns and gradually won their cooperation and support. You need to work with them not against them.

Participation in teaching and learning

At the beginning of each term, Ms Pauline and the other year teachers send a copy of the scheme of work to the parents for their feedback. The parents' comments are duly considered by the year teachers' team and where appropriate the schemes are modified accordingly. Parents also send their feedback on the teaching and learning process directly to the teacher in the home–school communication book. It is made clear from the beginning of the year that their feedback is welcomed as long as it is constructive and fair. Similarly, school and classroom rules about behaviour are sent to parents for approval before being enforced in the classroom.

Ms Pauline and her team involve the parents directly in classroom activities in areas in which parents may have particular expertise, such as music, drama, sports, crafts and exhibitions. In such instances, parents come and help directly in the classroom. Some parents had just helped set up a classroom exhibition for the whole-school on taking care of the environment. There were also plans at the whole-school level to include parents who had volunteered to work as classroom assistants in particular lessons, including Ms Pauline's class.

Besides the communication book, news from the classroom was reported in the school newsletter for parents which was published by the school bimonthly. Ms Pauline and her team were planning to start publishing their own (Year 4) parents' newsletter as well. One of the most useful aspects of this collaboration were the materials provided by parents to be used as teaching resources by Ms Pauline and her colleagues. Since parents and pupils would know beforehand the topics that were to be covered in the coming week/s, the pupils regularly brought charts, posters, books, software and educational games to be used by Ms Pauline in the lessons. On many occasions Ms Pauline did not need to spend any time in making her own resources. Moreover, since these were brought by the pupils themselves, they served to enhance the pupils' interest and engagement in the learning activities.

Case study 7.3 Parents as active partners in the life of the school

Parents had a very busy schedule at Red Robin Primary. They participated actively in school events, organised activities themselves and had frequent exchanges with the administration and the staff. They provided material and resources which teachers could use in their lessons. They were very active in raising funds for teaching and learning projects and for the embellishment of the school environment, in organising whole-school events such as concerts and excursions, and in holding personal development sessions for themselves. The following excerpt from a school document underlines the school's appreciation of their contribution:

> Parental involvement in the school has been abundant and varied, ranging from organising school activities to helping teachers produce teaching materials, or from decorating school corridors to the building of an adventure play-ground... Plans are now being considered to strengthen parent–teacher bonds by providing more opportunities for them to meet and possibly developing some form of teaching support service.

An audit report at the end of the year listed parental support, cooperation and interest as one of the strengths of the school. The school administration repeatedly referred to the 'excellent and very supportive' relationship between parents, staff and administration, underlining their cooperation and effort during public occasions, and awarding them a certificate of appreciation during Prize Day. Parents were also consulted on decisions made by the school and by the teachers. The schemes of work and other school policies were sent beforehand to the parents for their feedback. The school's code of behaviour, an excellent document which served as a prototype for other primary schools, was devised by a working group formed from a number of teachers and parents. Parents were also very active in the School Council and their participation was not a cosmetic one as the following school document affirms:

> Our School Council takes upon itself the duty of deciding major school policies and drawing up plans for their imple-mentation; and it can be frankly said that through its initia-tive, many positive changes and innovations have come to be born...it has been an effective means of rallying wide parental support for any school initiatives and activities.

Box 7.1 Collaborative learning

The following questions may help you to examine your practice in relation to cooperative learning in the classroom:

1. How would you describe the learning environment in your classroom in terms of competition/individualism/collaboration?

2. What structures and activities are there in the classroom which encourage pupils to listen to each other, engage in perspective taking, discuss and make decisions together, solve problems collectively and resolve conflict constructively?

3. How regular and frequent are cooperative learning activities usually held in your classroom? Do they occur in the majority of subjects or in a number of subjects only? Do you find that cooperative learning activities are suitable for particular subjects only or that they can be integrated in the mainstream classroom activities?

4. How do you support the pupils during cooperative learning activities to ensure that they are indeed working and learning collaboratively?

5. To what extent are the pupils engaging in more collaborative behaviour in the classroom as a result of such activities? Which particular behaviours are indicative that the pupils are indeed becoming more cooperative in their learning?

6. Which areas may need to be improved to promote more cooperative learning? For instance, are there pupils or groups of pupils who prefer to compete with each other or are reluctant to work with others? What can you do to encourage more cooperative behaviour in learning?

Box 7.2 Staff collaboration

The following exercise will help you examine the nature of your collaboration with your colleagues at the school.

1. In which of the following areas do you collaborate actively with the other members of the staff? Give examples of such collaboration for each area listed below.

2. What formal and informal structures are in place at your school to facilitate collaboration in these areas? Which of these do you make use of when engaged in collaboration in the areas listed below?

Curricular planning:

Curricular review:

Use of resources:

Scheme of work:

Pupil evaluation:

Code of behaviour:

Shared teaching:

Behaviour management:

For each item, put an X by the current situation/attitude and an O by the number you would have liked to see the situation in. The space between the X and the O is an indication of whether actions/changes in attitude are necessary or not. 1 means little or not often, 5 means a lot or frequent.	1	2	3	4	5
1	It is my responsibility to create a link between the class and the parents					
2	I'm good at interviewing techniques and giving information					
3	I find it necessary to work closely with the parents so that the pupils can develop their skills					
4	I consider collaborating with parents an important part of my work					
5	My expectations towards collaboration are clear					
6	I contact the parents regularly without a special reason					
7	I invite parents to visit and help with class work					
8	I talk with the parents about the pupils' strengths and weaknesses					
9	I contact the parents when their child is doing well					
10	I have introduced the school's policy on home–school collaboration					
11	I organise the collaboration together with the parents					
12	I prefer to work alone					
13	It is all right if not all the parents do not work equally with the classroom teacher					
14	I ask for the parents' help to evaluate the collaboration					
15	I feel insecure teaching when parents are visiting					
16	I enjoy working with parents					

Scoring and interpretation:
For each item, if X and O are side by side, score 1 point, if there is one column between them, score 2 points, two columns 3 points and three columns 4 points. What pattern emerges about your current situation in contrast to the desired one? Which are the areas which need to be improved? What changes do you need to make to bring about such an improvement?

Figure 7.1: Home–school collaboration (from Eggertsdottir *et al.* 2005)

Points for reflection

1. How collaborative is pupil engagement in the classroom? What opportunities and structures are provided for pupils to work and learn together? In which activities is this most and least evident? Box 7.1 may help you to answer these questions.

2. How collaborative would you describe your relationship with the other members of staff in your classroom, year group and school as a whole? In which area/s is it most and least evident? What structures and opportunities are in place to facilitate staff collaboration at your school? Box 7.2 may help you answer these questions.

3. How would you describe your relationship with the parents of your pupils? What strategies do you use to communicate with them? What opportunities do parents have to participate actively in the academic and social life of the classroom? Figure 7.1 may help you answer these questions.

4. On the basis of your assessment of classroom collaboration and collaboration with staff and parents, what goals would you like to set to improve your current practice? How can they be achieved? Did you find any of the examples listed above by the teachers helpful? Which of these do you think will be most useful to you in seeking to create more cooperative learning in the classroom and more teamwork with staff and parents?

SUMMARY

- The dominant approach to teaching and learning in many classrooms is still based on competition and individual achievement, yet research has repeatedly shown that cooperation in the classroom is superior to approaches in academic and social outcomes.

- In collaborative classrooms, the pupils exhibit higher levels of learning, have more positive relationships with teachers and peers, engage in more prosocial behaviour and develop more positive views of themselves. They feel more satisfied, are more accepted and supported by their peers and are more committed to their group and task.

- Cooperation is not limited to pupils in the classroom but to collaboration between pupils and teacher, between teacher and learning support assistants and among teachers themselves.

- Staff teamwork does not only lead to more effective teaching, with teachers more satisfied in their work and more committed to the school's objectives, but it contributes directly to classroom collaboration as well, setting role models in collaboration for all classroom members.

- Parents are important collaborative partners in the teaching and learning processes. Their involvement in the classroom is becoming more visible and meaningful.

- Classroom teachers who promote collaboration among their pupils, while they themselves engage in collaborative partnerships with their colleagues and parents, help to create a climate where pupils can thrive, grow and develop their educational and social competencies.

FURTHER READING

Aronson, E. and Patnoe, S. (1997) *The Jigsaw Classroom: Building Cooperation in the Classroom*. New York: Addison Wesley Longman.

Bryk, A., Camburn, E. and Louis, K.L. (1999) 'Professional community in Chicago Elementary School: facilitating factors and organizational consequences.' *Educational Administration Quarterly 35*, Supplement, 751–781. Available at www.eric.ed.gov/ERICDocs/data/ericdocs2sql/ content_storage_01/0000019b/80/15/02/76.pdf (accessed 22 November 2007).

Crozier, G. and Reay, D. (eds) (2005) *Activating Participation: Parents and Teachers Working Towards Partnership*. Stoke on Trent: Trentham Books.

Jarzabkowski, L.M. (1999) *Commitment and Compliance: Curious Bedfellows in Teacher Collaboration*. Available at www.aare.edu.au/99pap/jar99227.htm (accessed 12 December 2007).

Johnson, D.W. and Johnson, R. T. (1999) *Learning Together and Alone: Cooperative, Competitive and Individualistic Learning*. Boston: Allyn and Bacon.

Johnson, D.W., Johnson, R.T. and Stanne, M.B. (2000) *Cooperative Learning Methods: A Meta Analysis*. Available at www.co-operation.org/pages/cl-methods.html (accessed 22 November 2007).

McCarthey, S.J. (2000) 'Home–school connections: a review of the literature.' *Journal of Educational Research 93*, 3, 145–153.

McLaughlin, M.W. and Talbert, J. (2006) *Building School-Based Teacher Learning Communities*. New York: Teachers College Press.

Vincett, K., Cremin, H. and Thomas, G. (2005) *Teachers and Assistants Working Together*. Buckingham: Open University Press.

Willis, J. (2007) 'Cooperative learning is a brain turn-on.' *Middle School Journal 38*, 4, 4–13. Available at www.eric.ed.gov/ERICDocs/data/ericdocs2sql/content_storage_01/0000019b/80/2b/35/0f.pdf (accessed 22 November 2007).

CHAPTER 8

Empowering Classrooms: Choice, Voice and Belief

This final chapter in Part 2 addresses another facet of classroom engagement related to resilience building: influential participation in the classroom. This chapter discusses the pupils' basic need for autonomy and how this may be fulfilled in classrooms characterised by choice, voice and positive beliefs and expectations. The first section focuses on illustrations of pupils engaged in self-directing learning. The second part provides portraits of classrooms with pupils sharing responsibility with their teachers and participating in decisions about their learning and behaviour. The final section illustrates how pupils may become more confident and competent learners once teachers promote positive beliefs and set high but achievable expectations. The chapter ends with a number of reflective activities where you are invited to examine pupils' voice and choice and classroom beliefs, and make suggestions on how to create a more empowering context for the pupils.

> When they come to us in Year 4...they would have lost a lot of their individuality... They are used to do what they are told and to a way of working which has eroded their individuality; it is as if I am teaching one photocopy of another. (Ms Sunta)

Ms Sunta's frustration expressed above may come as no surprise for those of us who have experienced classrooms bent on control and compliance with little space for independent and creative thinking and learning. Schools and classrooms have traditionally been organised around uniformity and conformity with established rules and norms set by staff. Authority has been exercised largely by adults, and compliance praised and rewarded as a model of good behaviour, achievement and citizenship. Indeed, schools may be more willing to promote competence and success among pupils than autonomy and independent learning.

Of the four basic psychological needs of relatedness, competence, fun and autonomy, autonomy is usually the one which is most likely to be ignored in schools and classrooms (Osterman 2000). Yet research in past decades has shown that this 'sound' educational approach may be missing the whole point in seeking to promote the development of responsible and autonomous citizens. The use of controlling strategies such as lack of consultation, freedom and autonomy in the classroom has been found to be associated with competitive relationships among peers, misbehaviour and disengagement (Chirkov and Ryan 2001; Manke 1997; Solomon *et al.* 1992). In contrast, pupils in classes with autonomy-supportive teachers show more intrinsic motivation and perceived competence, become more engaged in learning activities and prosocial behaviour, and develop better relationships with peers and teachers (Chirkov and Ryan 2001; Manke 1997; Wentzel 1997).

> Teachers often say that they wish their pupils were more responsible. But this can turn into a moral complaint rather than a plan for improvement. If we want to understand and develop more self-directed learners, it's most productive to focus on what such a learner can do. (Watkins 2003, p.24)

The classrooms observed in this study were more focused on caring and support-ive relationships, active, meaningful and inclusive engagement, prosocial behav-iour and collaboration, with less attention paid to pupils' autonomy and self-directed behaviour. Despite a relatively weaker voice and limited choices, however, there were various examples of good practice, with pupils having choices about personal goals related to their learning and behaviour. This chapter captures some of these moments, highlighting three asects of this process: choice (opportunities to engage in self-directed learning); voice (opportunities to partici-pate in decisions); and belief (positive beliefs and expectations).

CHOICE
Autonomy within an ethic of care

It may sound paradoxical that while, on the one hand, pupils demand freedom and independence, on the other they need close and protective relationships with significant adults. Yet these twin needs can coexist, and classrooms may operate as contexts promoting both a sense of affiliation and a sense of autonomy (Olsen and Cooper 2001). Pupils need to feel safe and comfortable in their classrooms and they need structure and order to facilitate their learning. Those structures, however, have to be flexible enough to provide space and opportunity for pupils to set their own goals, make decisions and feel in control of their learning and behaviour. Ms Pauline explains how she first starts to build caring relationships within clear boundaries where pupils feel safe and are clear about expectations. She provides more opportunities for voice and choice once the ethic of care has been established. It is not the case of autonomy following relatedness; rather of autonomy becoming more salient as relatedness becomes more established:

> You know what we teachers used to say, hold on tight until Christmas, then start loosening your grip gradually in the new year. I do not follow this blindly, but I emphasise expectations in the beginning and make sure that these are clearly understood. I believe pupils first need to feel comfortable and secure in the classroom and also to make sure they are understanding and following the lessons. Then I give them more room to work on their own and I start to spend less time with pupils who are able to move on their own and dedicate more time with pupils who need support. Now [third term], for instance, they have more choices, whom to work with, choosing their own extra work, choosing themes for projects. I avoid spoonfeeding and encourage them to be creative in finding solutions. I give pupils more chance to choose how to behave according to consequence, so I am not trying to control them but to help them to become more responsible. They know what are the consequences and they can make their choices. Once pupils feel loved and accepted, they are more ready to accept the consequences of their behaviour. But as I said earlier on, I involve the pupils in deciding on work and behaviour rules from the first week; we set the classroom rules together.

An 'autonomy-ready' class

Ms Jane explained that with this year's group she felt she could risk giving pupils more choice and a stronger voice in the classroom. In doing so, she made the pupils her 'allies' in the teaching and learning process (cf. Houghton 2001):

> How much choice you give them depends on the group you have. This year I have a very mature group, it is one of the best groups I can remember; they are very mature for their age, very motivated and hardworking, very well behaved. They want to learn so much. I discuss a lot with them and involve them in what we are going to do and how we are going to do it. Yes, we have the syllabus and this year we have final examinations, and there is pressure from parents, so you are limited in how much freedom in work you can give. When we are going to do a new topic, I encourage them to do their own research at home [there is a good local library which pupils use very frequently] and they come and share their projects with the whole class; they make very good presentations. During the time for extra work, they can do independent reading or other related work, making use of books from what we have here in the lending library or from the school library or from home. During group work, I give them time to work and

find the solutions together...the groups they form themselves. In the beginning I choose who will be in each group but later during the year they divide themselves according to whom they feel they could work best with... Some time ago, we had a problem in this class with the behaviour of a particular boy. I did not try to solve the problem myself, but asked them to find a solution themselves as a group. We did a session all together and after many discussions they found a good solution. It is important that they learn from an early age to become more responsible and to find their own solutions to problems. (Ms Jane)

I like it when we make a mistake and we have to do it again, instead of the teacher giving me the answer, and similarly when we go to help others with their work, we also don't give them the answer...and in extra work we just do it ourselves, the teacher tells us: 'You don't need to come to me.' (Jeremy, a pupil in Ms Sunta's class)

A teacher-dependent class

Ms Veronica on the other hand had a hard task guiding the pupils to think for themselves and take more responsibility for their learning. They needed continuous guidance in learning and solving problems and she had to provide more structure and support than usual:

They used to come and ask me about whether to draw a line, write the date, skip a line or 'Miss I don't know how to do it...' It took time until they could start working without asking questions all the time. They are still young but I have been teaching this year for a number of years and I remember better classes than this. Now it is better, they are more independent in their work...what helped was that I insisted that they keep trying again and I sent them back to give it another try or to consult with their peers first. I also involved them in the lessons, choosing familiar topics, doing role plays, using attractive resources; in this way they felt more confident. What also helped was to ask them questions to help them to think and solve the problem, rather than giving them the answer. Yesterday, Mandy was stuck when writing a story on a shopping day at the city, so I asked her to think of the last time she went shopping with her mother. She liked the idea and we came up with the idea of drawing a map of the city centre with different points she could remember such as the bus station, the coffee shop, the shopping arcade, her mother's favourite shop, and so on. The idea was to provide her a scaffold which helped her to continue working on her own.

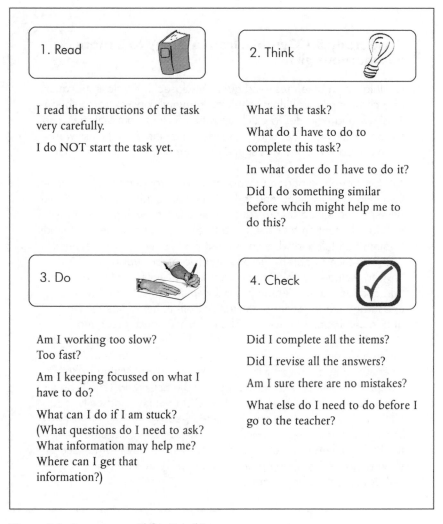

Figure 8.1: A prompt card for Cynthia

VOICE
Sharing responsibility in the classroom

The decentralisation process in education made it possible for schools to begin to participate in shaping their own destinies and running their own affairs. In the great majority of cases, schools are still run by adults, with pupils being the least enfranchised group; but gradually pupils are finding that their voices are being heard, even in circles which were traditionally out of bounds for them. Nowadays they have a right to have a say and their voice is listened to and considered. When they are consulted about the goals which will determine the kind of activities

Case study 8.1 Cynthia: from a clingy to a more autonomous girl

Cynthia was a quiet, reserved girl in Ms Josephine's class. Because of a chronic physical illness she was frequently absent from school. As she found it harder to catch up with the classroom activities, she became clingy and dependent on Ms Josephine during class work. During break time she was spending more and more time on her own.

Ms Josephine began to work on a two-pronged plan to support Cynthia in her learning and to facilitate her social inclusion with her peers. She drew up an educational programme with provisions for individual attention by herself and by Simone, one of the few friends Cynthia had left and who was seated next to her. A buddy system was introduced whereby Simone and two other pupils took it in turns to include Cynthia during play. Once Cynthia felt more secure and confident in her learning, Ms Josephine's next target was to encourage her to take more initiative both in her academic work and in her social interactions. She modelled various learning strategies which then Cynthia could make use of on her own. She made a simple card with four boxes with questions to be asked when carrying out an activity. The card instructed Cynthia to READ carefully the instructions before starting the activity, to THINK on what she had to and how to do it, to DO the task and finally to CHECK and revise the work completed (see Figure 8.1). In this way she was being trained to work more independently. Together with the PSD teacher and a circle of friends, Ms Josephine organised a short social skills training programme to develop Cynthia's self-esteem and assertiveness.

held in the classroom, how such activities will be organised and evaluated, how they are expected to behave and the consequences of their behaviour, pupils make an investment in their own learning. What is taking place makes more sense and has more meaning; they work harder and take more responsibility for their own learning and behaviour (Cook-Sather 2002; Wilson and Corbett 2001).

> Pupils in our class work hard and pay attention and do their best, even slow ones do their best… I like that…we don't miss lessons… We learn so much here…they teach us everything, even Year 5 and Year 6 material… There are many pupils who want to learn not because they are forced to and pushed by the teachers. (A group of pupils in Ms Gertrude's class)

A framework for assessing pupils' views of themselves as independent learners (Watkins 2003)

How do pupils view their learning experiences in your classroom? How much do they feel they are in control of their own learning? How much autonomy do they feel they have? The following questionnaire will assist you in examining the pupils' views on the learning process. It will be completed by the pupils in your class either individually or as a group.

	We are interested in your views about learning. There are no 'right' or 'wrong' answers. Can you tell us how you approach your learning? Just put a tick in one of the columns on the right for each item.	*Strongly agree*	*Agree*	*Disagree*	*Strongly disagree*
1	Before I start my work, I work out the best way to do it				
2	I can do my best even if I don't like what the lesson is about				
3	When my teacher gives hints on how best to do something, I will try them out				
4	I sometimes ask myself 'Am I going about this in the best way?'				
5	I know when I have understood something when I can say it in my own words				
6	If I find something difficult in class, I talk to the teacher				
7	I do not ask questions in class				

Figure 8.2: Pupils' views of themselves as independent learners

continued on next page

8	When I am reading I sometimes stop to make sure I am understanding				
9	With a new topic I can usually find something interesting to learn				
10	When I get new work, I jump straight in and sometimes wish I hadn't				
11	When I do not understand something in a lesson, I ask a classmate				

Scoring and interpretation:
What pattern emerges about pupils' sense of being in charge of their learning? What strengths in this area could be celebrated and maintained? What aspects need to be improved? What changes do you need to make to bring about such an improvement?

NB. If a score were to be derived from responses to these items, numbers 7 and 10 would need to be reverse-scored.

Scoring and interpretation:
What pattern emerges about pupils' learning orientation in your class? What are the strengths of this group? What aspects need to be improved? What changes do you need to make to bring about such an improvement?
NB. If a score were to be derived from responses to these items, numbers 11 to 20 would need to be reverse scored.

Figure 8.2: Pupils' views of themselves as independent learners *continued*

Including what pupils like

Ms Veronica describes how despite the constraints imposed by a set national minimum curriculum, a culture underlining staff authority in school and the young age of her pupils, she sought to give pupils some say in the classroom decisions:

> My group is still young, mostly six- and seven-year-olds, and they are not used to discussing what the teacher is going to do. As you know we have a national minimum curriculum which limits our choices on the topics to be covered over the year. However, I try to be as flexible as possible, adjusting the themes to needs of the pupils rather than pushing on with the syllabus. In this way the pupils are having an indirect choice in the type of activities I do for them. I also try to include activities which they like and use them again in the future, and avoid activities they do not like. I use role play a

great deal; when we did it the first time, they really enjoyed it and were very excited and asked me to do it again. They also like to work in groups, so I include one small group activity or more every day. Another thing I found they like is when they bring pictures, books, toys and other material from home and share them with the class. Sometimes I use them in the lesson. They like jokes, so I include some humour, even if sometimes they keep going on. When they finish their work, I also let them do an activity of their choice as long as it is related to the topic. Another thing they like is to work on the project-of-the-week scrapbook, or to read story books which they bring with them and share with each other. Sometimes I let them work with a partner or group of their choice for particular activities; this though does not always work as some pupils do not work when they pair up or they disrupt the group. So it depends; I try to find a balance between what I have to do and what they like and dislike.

Including pupils in evaluation

Ms Pauline had attended a European workshop on classroom assessment and she had become the point of reference at the school on assessment. She complained about the national 'competence-proving' system of assessment, with its focus on performance, tests and end-of-year examinations leading to selection and stream-ing. Parallel with the national examinations, however, she developed her own 'competence-improving' assessment scheme together with the pupils. She devel-oped a portfolio for each pupil that listed all the achievements and improvements:

> I don't like pupils competing with each other for grades. I discourage them from doing it and emphasise that we learn together. For instance, during group work I give a group rather than an individual score. I am careful with using the red biro too often; I try to give feedback from which they could learn as pupils have to know what they did right and what was wrong, that is how they learn. I try to involve the pupils in corrections as well. Homework is corrected by the pupils themselves following a class model. I am at the moment working on a self-assessment scheme to be used in some of the activities. It is based on giving the pupils a set of questions which they would have to answer once they finish the activity and before they come to me for correction. The questions include 'What was I expected to do in this task? How well have I done it? How many correct answers do I think there are? How many mistakes do I think there are? Which are these and what can I do about them? What have I learned from it?' In this way they would know beforehand what they have to do and what is the goal of the activity and what they need to ask themselves to see if they have achieved the learning objective. When they are ready with the evaluation, they give themselves a score or a grade according to how many are correct, or how many mistakes there are or if they completed so many items. When I correct their work, we then compare our feedback and our grades. I

already tried it in maths, but they need more coaching and time to get used to working in this way. You cannot just go and ask them to do it. Our system is too exam-oriented, so you need to slowly train the pupils to start working in this way.

Case study 8.2 Examining pupils' views on learning

Ms Gertrude's class was participating in a whole-school initiative on examining pupils' views on learning. With the help of an outside consultant each class had a one-hour session discussing their learning, what they liked and did not like, what helped them and did not help them to learn, which teacher strategies facilitated or did not facilitate learning. During the activity the class teacher left the classroom so that the pupils could feel safe to express their opinions openly. At the end each class had to come up with two suggestions for what helped them to learn in the classroom and two suggestions for what might help them learn more. These suggestions were then discussed by the school consultant and the respective class teachers to see how they could be implemented in the classroom. This was a pilot project and the school was considering how it could be turned into a regular self-evaluation exercise, such as through the use of a Critical Friend and peer reviews. Ms Gertrude found that this activity helped her to fine-tune and improve her practice:

> I was particularly surprised by one of their suggestions – they suggested less teacher talk and more interaction. It is my style to involve them in the lesson as much as I can, to do a lot of discussions, but it seems that I have been talking and chalking more than I had realised. This helped me to be more on my guard. I was talking with one of my colleagues and we thought that the next year we could give feedback to each other; we could go to each other's class and then share our thoughts on what we think may be improved.

Involving pupils in regulating their own and the classroom behaviour

Ms Erica sees the pupils as 'minor collaborative partners'. At the beginning of the scholastic year she holds a Circle Time session to establish a set of classroom rules for the coming year. Together the group discusses how every classroom member is expected to behave and agrees on a set of behaviours which applies to all and are agreed by all. The focus is on a small number of simple and practical behaviours which are easily understood by all the pupils, such as completing set work or listening to each other (see the set of behaviours of Ms Erica's class for this year in Case study 8.3). Ms Erica ensures that she herself observes the behaviours (or equivalent behaviours) in order to set a role model for the pupils. The rationale for the behaviours is explained so that all pupils appreciate that it is in their own and their peers' interest that the rules are observed. When pupils listen to the teacher during explanations, for instance, they will know what they have to do, their peers will be able to follow the explanation without distractions and the teacher will not to have to keep repeating explanations all over again.

The group also discusses the rewards for the observation of the behaviours and the sanctions to be applied when the rules are broken, with the emphasis on rewards and behaviour learning rather than punishment. The set of behaviours are given to the parents so that they can support the class in observing the behaviours, particularly home-related behaviours (e.g. arriving on time, bringing homework and material for learning). A chart of the set rules is displayed in a prominent place in the classroom. It is made clear from the beginning that some rules are not negotiable, either because these are school rules agreed by the whole school community (e.g. coming to school on time or coming to school in uniform), or because they may be harmful to the pupils (e.g. violent behaviour is not tolerated). When conflicts arise, the agreed rules are used as a framework for conflict resolution, with all partners concerned having a right of reply.

During the first mid-term in November the class reviews the rules during another Circle Time session and makes any modifications which are considered necessary to ensure maximum observation. The success of Ms Erica's approach is that it involves the pupils directly in their own learning and regulation of behaviour. It sets clear expectations about learning and behaviour which are agreed and owned by the whole classroom, it emphasises behaviour for learning and it makes provisions for supporting pupils in the learning process within a caring climate.

Box 8.1 The five rules of Ms Erica's classroom

Working and learning together

1. We listen to the teacher during explanations.
2. We complete our work in class.
3. We bring all the material we need for learning.
4. We help each other with our work in class.
5. We listen to each other when we have a problem between us.

A classroom parliament

Ms Erica explains how she got the idea of setting up a classroom parliament after some pupils from the school visited the national parliament where they had the opportunity to sit on the Members of Parliament's seats and put questions to the speaker, the Prime Minister, the Ministers and the Leader of the Opposition. It was a rewarding, empowering experience, and she sought to give her pupils a similar opportunity.

The classroom parliament consists of five pupils elected by their peers for one 'term' (half a school term) (the next parliament will have new members so that more pupils will have the opportunity to sit in parliament). Parliament holds regular informal meetings with the class teacher and more formal but less frequent meetings involving the whole class, with the other peers 'in the strangers' gallery'. The brief of the parliament is to improve the teaching and learning process, such as the classroom environment, classroom activities and homework, relationships, classroom rules and social activities. With regard to small decisions, such as how to keep the class clean, voting will be cast only by the five members and the teacher, but in more important issues such as how to structure classroom activities of deciding the amount of homework, a referendum can be held involving the whole class. Ms Erica has the right to veto any decision, but she uses this power only when no other solution can be found and when she thinks that the behaviour being proposed may be inappropriate (e.g. no homework).

The members of parliament keep a very close relationship with their 'constituents' and many of the issues raised in the parliamentary sessions are indeed suggested by the other pupils through a standard question sheet. An anonymous question box is also used and the suggestions are discussed by the members to decide whether to put the question/issue on the agenda. The rules of Circle Time are applied during the sessions, such as sitting in two concentric circles, listening to each other and treating each other with respect, dealing with one issue at a time, with sessions lasting about half an hour. Ms Erica had to be very directive in the beginning, taking more the role of the Speaker to keep order and to make sure that parliament could function. With time she has given more power to the members and has had to use her veto less. The initial minor issues such as 'a more attractive classroom environment' gradually gave way to more serious concerns, such as passing a law on bullying and introducing peer support in the class. Ms Erica described the initiative as demanding but worth the effort. The pupils became more engaged and enthusiastic, they participated more in classroom activities, their relationships and behaviour improved, there was less quarrelling and fighting, and pupils felt more confident in communicating their ideas.

Box 8.2 Pupil rights in the classroom

Pupil rights at Red Robin Primary School

- We have the right to be ourselves and be respected for who we are
- We have the right to learn
- We have the right to feel safe and secure
- We have the right to express ourselves in a safe environment
- We have the right to be supported when needed
- We have the right to be included and to participate in the activities of our school

(adapted from the school's code of behaviour)

A charter of pupil rights in the classroom

- *I have the right to be safe in this room.* This means no one will hit me, kick me, punch me, pinch me, or hurt me.
- *I have the right to be happy and to be treated with compassion in this room.* This means that no one will laugh at me or hurt my feelings.
- *I have the right to learn in this room.* This means that I am free to express my feelings without being interrupted or punished.
- *I have the right to be heard and to hear in this room.* This means that no one will shout, yell, scream, or make loud noises.
- *I have the right to be myself in this room.* This means that no one will treat me unfairly because of my appearance, gender, abilities, or background.

(Saskatchewan Education, 1995)

BELIEF
Promoting positive beliefs and high expectations
Instilling self-efficacy and optimism among pupils...

One of the ways teachers communicated the belief that pupils had what it took to be successful was their affirmation of pupils' skills and ability and their insistence with the pupils that they could do better if they tried harder. Rogers (1998) labelled these beliefs 'prescriptive', representing optimistic views of the pupils in contrast to the more deterministic 'probabilistic' expectations based on what teachers believed was likely to happen.

Ms Gertrude sought to 'wring' the best out of her pupils by repeatedly encouraging and challenging them to work and study harder, and by building on their ideas and strengths during the lessons. She frequently told the pupils that she and others were impressed by their hard work and progress. When other members of staff, parents or professionals visited the classroom, she always made it a point to underline the good qualities of the pupils, expressing her satisfaction and pride at their hard work, motivation and learning. She helped to establish a positive and optimistic belief in the learning ability of the pupils, raising expectation and developing the identity of a competent, hardworking and successful group. She worked very hard herself, preparing material, taking work home, showing a high level of energy and enthusiasm during lessons, consulting with colleagues and taking an active interest in the pupils, all of which served as an inspiration for the pupils themselves. The pupils were given the opportunity to contribute actively to the activities and they frequently shared their work, projects and knowledge on particular topics with each other. Ms Gertrude used the pupils as classroom resources, making use of their stories, projects and skills during the lessons. Such a climate instilled a sense of academic efficacy among the pupils leading to more effort and success. They learned to believe more in themselves as efficacious and capable learners. Pupils who believe that they and their group are good, able and competent learners are more likely to become engaged in the tasks presented, even if such tasks may appear challenging, to give their best in such tasks, to try out new and challenging tasks, and to persist in the face of obstacles and difficulty (Bandura 1993; Linnenbrink and Pintrich 2003).

...including the 'weaker' pupils

One of the challenges for the classroom teacher is to hold high expectations not only for the achieving pupils, but also for those with learning difficulties. Ms Sunta's class was a mixed ability class in a school with a relatively high level of pupils coming from disadvantaged social backgrounds. She had a number of pupils with learning and behavioural difficulties. She believed that she and the school were instrumental in bringing about effective change in the children entrusted to them, even if such children came from families or communities in difficulty. She believed that she could make a difference in the lives of children facing all sorts of challenges, and that conviction, coupled with her love of teaching and love of children, gave her the energy she needed to give her best for the pupils. The common expectation in her class was that all pupils had the potential to learn, each according to his or her ability, reflecting the common classroom value of learning for all. She remarked that she expected all pupils in her class to achieve despite any differences, proudly mentioning how two pupils who had previously experienced considerable difficulties in their learning were now showing remarkable progress. She underlined the need to instil belief and hope in the pupils in the face of potential failure:

When they come to us in Year 4, they are already set and some have already given up. They have a hard struggle to unlearn what they had learnt, that they are not good. This is one of the battles I have.

One of the weapons Ms Sunta uses in her 'battle' is the development of self-enhancing attributions among the pupils. Through her language, behaviour and practice, she underlines her conviction that all pupils can learn and achieve, that success is largely dependent on their efforts and that their past history of failure is related to lack of effort support and belief in oneself. This resonates with what one pupil from her class remarked, and underlines the motivational value of teachers' optimistic belief in pupils' potential, attributing success to effort and failure to external factors:

> One of the things the teacher tells us all the time is to try things out, not to give up. She tells us, 'If there is a difficult sum, you have to win not the sum'. We must not be afraid, we have to use our brains...and when it is examination time, she tells us not to be afraid... I had many difficulties in Year 1 and Year 3 but with this Miss I have made a great improvement.

High expectations encourage pupils to accept challenges which lead to experiences of success, but only if they're 'do-able', and if teachers support pupils in fulfilling the expectations without putting undue pressure on them. As described above, Ms Sunta did not expect all her pupils to move at the same pace and level or to compete with each other for the best pupil or the first prize. The expectations were tailored according to the pupils' readiness level and the pupils provided with 'purposeful support' (Krovetz 1999) to reach these expectations. She employed multi-level, multi-modal teaching techniques, with various forms of support and resources. These have already been described in Chapter 6. Clearly, teachers' beliefs about themselves as teachers, and about their pupils' abilities and motivations and the likelihood of their pupils' success, can shape the quality of their interactions with pupils as well as the quality of their instructions.

> For children...used to thinking of themselves as stupid [and] not worth talking to...a good teacher can provide an astonishing revelation. [She] can give a child at least a chance to feel, 'She thinks I'm worth something; maybe I am.' (Kidder 1990, p.3)

Points for reflection

1. To what extent are pupils in your classroom in charge of their learning? What choices do they have in setting learning goals, in the way they learn, in the type of tasks they engage in, in the evaluation of their products, and in pursuing their own interests? Figure 8.2 may help you to evaluate pupils' views of themselves as autonomous learners.

2. To what extent are pupils actively involved in the decisions made in the classroom? Do they have a voice in the way they learn and behave? What structures are in place to facilitate pupils' participation in decisions? Use Figure 8.3 to help you answer this question.

3. How would you describe your beliefs and expectations about your pupils' learning potential, including pupils considered at risk? What strategies do you use to promote the belief and expectation that all pupils can learn? What beliefs and expectations do the pupils hold of themselves as learners? How confident and competent do they feel? Use Figure 8.4 to help you with these questions.

4. On the basis of your assessment of pupil autonomy and influence, what goals would you like to set in your classroom to improve your current practice? How can these goals be achieved? Did you find any of the examples listed above by the teachers helpful? Which of these do you think will be most useful to you in seeking to create a more empowering context promoting choice, voice and positive beliefs and expectations?

A framework for assessing pupils' influence in the classroom (Cefai 2008)

What say do pupils have in your classroom? Do they take an active participation in decisions related to learning goals, learning activities, ways of working, task evaluation, classroom rules and behaviour, and conflict resolution? The following checklist will assist you to examine the pupils' say in various aspects of the classroom life.

	To what extent do pupils in your classroom have a say in deciding on the following aspects of classroom life?	Never	Not very often	Usually	Always
1	Pursuing their own interests				
2	Setting their own learning goals				
3	Deciding on where to sit in the classroom				
4	Deciding on how the timetable is set for the day				
5	Deciding on whom to work with				
6	Deciding on which topics to learn				
7	Deciding on how the learning activities are structured and delivered				
8	Deciding on whether to work individually or in groups				
9	Deciding on the use and type of resources used in the activities				
10	Deciding on the type and nature of tasks set				
11	Deciding on the product to be presented				

Figure 8.3: Pupils' influence in the classroom

continued on next page

	To what extent do pupils in your classroom have a say in deciding on the following aspects of classroom life?	Never	Not very often	Usually	Always
12	Deciding on how their product is to be evaluated				
13	Deciding on the actual evaluation of their product				
14	Deciding on the amount, nature and evaluation of the homework				
15	Deciding on how rewards and recognition are given and presented				
16	Deciding on the classroom rules governing behaviour				
17	Deciding on the consequences in the application of the classroom rules				
18	Deciding on how the rules are reinforced, monitored and evaluated				
19	Deciding on how conflicts with peers and teacher are resolved				
20	Deciding on how classroom responsibilities are assigned				

Scoring and interpretation:
What pattern emerges about the level of pupils' involvement in classroom decisions? What strengths are to be celebrated and maintained? What aspects need to be improved? What changes do you need to make to bring about such an improvement?

Figure 8.3: Pupils' influence in the classroom *continued*

A framework for assessing pupils' views of themselves as competent and confident learners (Cefai 2008)

How do pupils see themselves as learners? What learning expectations do they have? How confident are they in their own ability to learn? The following questionnaire will assist you in examining the pupils' beliefs in this area. It will be completed by the pupils in your class either individually or as a group.

I am interested in your views about yourself as a learner. There are no 'right' or 'wrong' answers. Just put a tick in the column on the right for each item.

		Strongly agree	Agree	Disagree	Strongly disagree
1	My teacher thinks that I am a good and able pupil				
2	My peers think that I am a good and able pupil				
3	I believe that I am a good and able pupil				
4	I believe I will be successful in school				
5	I can learn and improve in all subjects if I work and study				
6	I can always learn if I try hard enough				
7	When there is something I don't know, I don't know what to do				
8	When I find something difficult, I try hard to find an answer				
9	When I don't know what to do, I give up and do something else				
10	When there is a difficult sum, I try and try again to get it				
11	When I do not know how to read a word, I go immediately to the next one				
12	I find it difficult to continue working when I don't know something				

Scoring and interpretation:
What pattern emerges about pupils' view of themselves as competent and confident learners? What strengths in this area may be celebrated and maintained? What aspects need to be improved? What changes do you need to make to bring about such an improvement?
NB. If a score were to be derived from responses to these items, numbers 7, 9 and 11 would need to be reverse-scored.

Figure 8.4: Pupils' confidence in learning

SUMMARY

- Pupils' need for autonomy appears to be the one most teachers tend to ignore in contrast to the needs for competence and relatedness.

- Autonomy, however, is a fundamental basic need in children and young people, and while they need to feel safe and comfortable in their classroom, they also need space and opportunity to set their own goals, make decisions and feel in control of their learning and behaviour.

- When provided with choice and voice in the classroom, pupils believe more in themselves as competent learners, participate actively in the learning activities, engage in more prosocial behaviour and develop better relationships with their teachers and peers.

- This basic need is satisfied when classrooms operate as empowering contexts for their pupils, providing regular and frequent opportunities to make choices in the way they learn and behave, to engaging in self-directed learning and behaviour, to participate in decisions, to believe in themselves as efficacious and competent learners and to set high but achievable expectations for themselves.

FURTHER READING

Areglado, R.J., Bradley, R.C. and Lane, P.S. (1996) *Learning for Life: Creating Classrooms for Self-Directed Learning.* Thousand Oaks, CA: Corwin Press.

Bandura, A. (1993) 'Perceived self efficacy in cognitive development and functioning.' *Educational Psychologist 28*, 2, 117–148.

Birenbaum, M. (2002) 'Assessing self-directed active learning in primary schools.' *Assessment in Education: Principles, Policy and Practice 90*, 1, 119–138.

DfES (2004) *Pupil Participation. Working Together: Giving Children and Young People a Say.* Available at www.teachernet.gov.uk/publications (accessed 22 November 2007).

Linnenbrink, E.A. and Pintrich, P.R. (2003) 'The role of self-efficacy in student engagement and learning in the classroom.' *Reading and Writing Quarterly: Overcoming Learning Difficulties 19*, 2, 119–137.

Macbeath, J., Demetriou, H., Rudduck, J. and Myers, K. (2003) *Consulting Pupils: A Toolkit for Teachers.* Cambridge: Pearson Publishing.

Palmer, S.B. and Wehmeyer, M.L. (2003) 'Promoting self-determination in early elementary school: teaching self-regulated problem-solving and goal-setting skills.' *Remedial and Special Education 24*, 2, 115–126.

Rowe, S. (n.d.) *A Journey Toward Self Directed Learning in Young Children.* Available at www.madison.k12.wi.us/sod/car/abstracts/355.pdf (accessed 22 November 2007).

Rudduck, J., Brown, N. and Hendy, L. (2004) *Personalised Learning and Pupil Voice: The East Sussex Project.* London: DfES. Available at www.teachernet.gov.uk/publications (accessed 22 November 2007).

Zimmerman, B.J. (2002) 'Becoming a self-regulated learner: an overview.' *Theory into Practice 41*, 2, 64–70.

PART 3

A PLAN OF ACTION FOR THE CLASSROOM PRACTITIONER

CHAPTER 9

A Plan of Action for Educational Resilience in the Classroom

This chapter presents a plan of action to help the practitioner implement the model presented in this book in his or her own classroom. An action research framework guides the classroom teacher, in consultation with pupils, parents and colleagues, to address the question 'How can the classroom be organised in such a way as to promote socio-emotional competence and educational engagement for all the pupils?' The process starts with an assessment of the various aspects of the classroom context, suggesting various tools and instruments to assist in the assessment. This is then followed by the formulation of a plan of action on the sheet provided, the implementation of the plan, evaluation and further action.

CHANGE FROM WITHIN: TEACHERS AS AGENTS OF CHANGE

This book proposes a positive view of classrooms fostering cognitive and socio-emotional competence for all pupils, away from deficit and blame approaches. It focuses attention on the importance of classroom relationships, on an ethic of care, support and inclusion. It underlines the need of pupils learning and working together, actively engaged in authentic activities related to life experiences. It suggests that classrooms organised as caring, inclusive, prosocial and learning-centred communities fulfil pupils' basic needs for affiliation, competence, autonomy and fun, consequently promoting their social and academic development. They protect pupils from the various risks they may be exposed to and steer their development towards more positive trajectories.

> It is better to appreciate the complexity of a problem or situation than to be seduced by simplistic remedies that cannot work. (after Eisner 1998)

Classroom communities can make a difference in children's and young people's lives. Change must, however, come from within the classroom itself, rather than imposed from above or outside. Presenting ready-made models and recipes with which classrooms can fix their problems or bring about innovations is likely to be a futile exercise, one transient innovation among many which would quickly end up in the bin (Fullan 1991). Any change has to be introduced in a way that fits in within the existing nature, culture and needs of each individual school and class-room community, building on pupils' and teachers' strengths and diversity. Those responsible for introducing changes need to be close to the process of change occurring in the classroom, to be able to engage in self-analysis and reflection. The onus of responsibility for creating resilience-enhancing classrooms is thus on the classroom members themselves. In partnership with the pupils, parents and staff, the classroom teachers are directed to examine their own classroom contexts and seek to bring about change according to their own needs, strengths and resources.

Action research provides an excellent framework for classroom practitioners in their resilience-enhancement efforts. It considers the classroom teacher, together with the pupils, parents and other members of staff, as the people best placed to understand and analyse the classroom situation and introduce, implement and evaluate new practices accordingly. It involves a cyclical process of systematically assessing what is happening in the classroom, implementing action to improve the situation, and monitoring and evaluating the effects of the action to ensure continuing improvement (Hopkins 2002). Action and reflection are carried out by the classroom members through an ongoing, collaborative, participative and critical process, examining and reflecting upon one's own and others' practices.

As noted earlier, the key question which needs to be addressed is: 'How can the classroom be organised in a way to promote socio-emotional competence and educational engagement among all the pupils?' There are four stages which will enable the classroom practitioner together with pupils, parents and colleagues to address this question. First, one needs to undertake an assessment of the classroom situation in order to develop a plan of action to improve what is already taking place. Next, the classroom teacher, together with pupils and parents as appropriate, puts the action plan into effect and monitors its implementation systematically. Finally, in the last two stages the classroom members review the impact and effectiveness of the plan, which may lead to further action to continue improving practice. This will bring the process back to implementation, observation, reflection and evaluation and back again to planning and imple-mentation. Figure 9.1 shows the cyclical nature of a classroom practitioner-led process in bringing about change in the classroom.

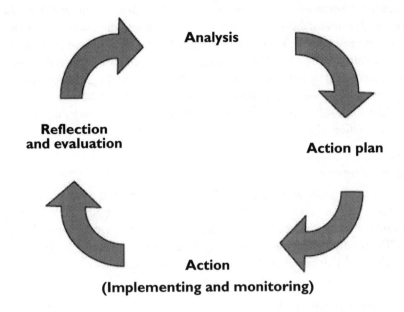

Figure 9.1: The action research cycle

STAGE 1   ANALYSIS FOR ACTION: WHERE ARE WE NOW?

The first stage in classroom resilience-building is to analyse the current classroom situation in order to define the goals of intervention and prepare a plan of action. This is not a summative, psychometric assessment undertaken by resilience consultants. It is a formative and dynamic analysis undertaken by the classroom practitioner in consultation with the pupils, parents and colleagues as part of a process of self-improvement and growth. It is a natural, systemic exercise close and sensitive to the ecological context of the classroom. The analysis focuses on what is actually happening, tapping the views of all those taking part in the classroom activities with a view to improving practice through a plan of action. This requires that the classroom teacher, together with pupils and parents, be empowered to carry out their own analysis in seeking to bring about change. This is an analysis of classroom processes, of the classroom relationships, activities, practices and beliefs, rather than a measurement of individual socio-emotional competence, learning or achievement. In line with the model presented in this book, change is possible by analysing the context where behaviour is taking place and seeking to strengthen, modify or emphasise the processes which have been found to support the socio-emotional competence and learning of the pupils in the classroom. Besides establishing targets for improvement, the analysis identifies areas which need to be celebrated and extended in the classroom. Furthermore, the analysis process can be built in and integrated into the curricular, pedagogical and interpersonal processes taking place in the daily life of the classroom. It may be organised as a feature of classrooms as self-reflective communities. Finally, rather than a one-off exercise, the assessment is dynamic and ongoing and the consequent action plan has inbuilt steps for continuous evaluation.

What to examine

The classroom features underlined in this book as promoting educational resilience relate to the various psychosocial processes making up the classroom community, namely classroom relationships, behaviours, practices, beliefs and values. The following framework may help the classroom practitioner to examine systematically the different aspects of classroom functioning.

Teacher–pupil relationship

How would you describe the relationship you have with the pupils in general? How do the pupils themselves perceive such a relationship? How caring and supportive is such a relationship? How safe, secure and supported do the pupils feel in the classroom? What evidence is there for this? What strategies are being actually used to establish a caring and nurturing relationship with the pupils? Which areas are working really well? Which need to be improved?

Classroom management

How would you describe your classroom management style? Is it fundamentally positive? What impact does it have on your relationship with the pupils? Are classroom rules agreed, positive, understood, accepted and based on rights and responsibilities? Are you modelling appropriate behaviour? Do you use alternative strategies to avoid unnecessary confrontation? Are pupils involved in negotiating solutions for conflicting situations? What strategies are in place to repair relationships following correction or conflict? How do pupils view your behaviour management style? Which areas are working really well? Which need to be improved?

Pupil relationships

How would you describe the social climate in the classroom? How do pupils relate to each other during classroom activities and during play? How harmonious, caring and supportive are these relationships? Are there any cliques, any neglected or rejected pupils? How is conflict and disagreement resolved between the classroom members? How do the members feel to be part of the group? What strategies are in place to create more harmonious and caring peer relationships in this class? Which areas are working really well? Which need to be improved?

Pupil engagement

How would you describe the nature and level of pupils' engagement in the classroom? How authentic and meaningful are the classroom activities for the pupils? What opportunities are there for pupils to be actively involved in the learning process? Is there a focus on learning rather than just on achievement? How do the pupils view their learning experiences? Is it fun to be a learner in this classroom? What strategies and resources are employed to engage pupils in the learning process? Which areas are working really well? Which need to be improved?

Pupil inclusion

Is the curriculum offered in this class accessible and appropriate for all the pupils? Does it promote learning for all pupils? Do the pedagogy, resources and assessment modes complement the various readiness levels and interests of the pupils? What modifications do you make to ensure accessibility and success for all? Are any classroom members disadvantaged because of any difference, and if yes, what is done to remove the barriers? Do all the pupils feel valued and respected members of the group? Which areas are working really well? Which need to be improved?

Pupil collaboration

How would you describe the classroom climate in terms of individuality, competition and collaboration? How cooperative and collaborative are pupils in their learning? Do they support one another, and if yes, in what way? What is the pupils' view about their classroom in this respect? What opportunities and structures are there to encourage pupils to learn and construct knowledge together? Which areas are working really well? Which need to be improved?

Pupil influence

How involved are pupils in the decisions made in the classroom? What choices do they have regarding academic and social behaviour? Are they consulted on decisions relating to what is taught, how it is taught and assessed, and how to behave in the classroom? What means are used to facilitate their voice in the classroom? What do pupils think about their voice in the classroom? Which areas are working really well? Which need to be improved?

Pupil autonomy

How would you describe the pupils' level of autonomy and self-reliance in learning? How is this manifested? What structures and practices are in place to facilitate opportunities for autonomy and self-directed learning and behaviour? What do the pupils think about their level of autonomy in the classroom? Which areas are working really well? Which need to be improved?

Positive beliefs and expectations; recognition

How would you describe the core values of this class? Do such values promote positive beliefs about all pupils' strengths and potential to learn? Are messages of hope and optimism present in your daily conversations and interactions with the pupils? Is there an expectation that all pupils are able to learn and achieve, each according to his or her readiness level, and that they would be supported to do so? Are high expectations evident for all pupils, including ones who are experiencing difficulty? How do you instil a sense of efficacy and positive belief among the pupils? What structures are in place to promote such beliefs? How do the pupils look at themselves as learners? Is there any group or individual who has negative views or expectations? Which areas are working really well? Which need to be improved?

Relationships with parents

How would you describe your relationship with the pupils' parents in general? How engaged are the parents in the classroom? How frequent is the communication between yourself and the parents? How supportive and collaborative are they? What influence do they have in the social and academic practices taking place in the classroom? Are they consulted on any decisions that are made? What structures are in place to facilitate the active engagement of the parents? Are there any parents who are disaffected or disengaged? How do parents view their own involvement and participation in the classroom? What are their views on the classroom? Which areas are working really well? Which need to be improved?

Relationships with colleagues

How would you describe the relationship with your colleagues at work? How collegial and collaborative is the relationship? Do you plan your work together, exchange views and practice, and support each other? What efforts do you make to ensure more collegial and collaborative relationships with peers? How helpful is this relationship in the development of your professional competence? Is there a sense of belonging among the staff? How do the rest of the staff feel about the sense of belonging, collegiality and teamwork at your school? What structures are in place to promote closer relationships among staff and to facilitate more teamwork? Which areas are working really well? Which need to be improved?

Whole-school participation

How involved are you in the life of the school? How participative are you in staff meetings and staff-development sessions? Do you participate regularly in social occasions organised by the school? How well informed are you about the school's policies? Are you making use of the physical and human resources available at the school to enhance your competence and support the learning and behaviour of your pupils? How would you describe your relationship with the school adminis-tration? How supportive is the administration in facilitating your work in the classroom? What can you do to improve the communication with the administra-tion? Which areas are working really well? Which need to be improved?

How to go about it

In answering the questions listed in the above framework, the classroom practi-tioner may make use of various techniques and strategies. Gathering information through various methods and from various sources, rather than relying on a single instrument used with one source, will help to provide a more holistic, detailed and in-depth portrait of the areas being examined.

Direct observation and reflection

Classroom observation may take various forms, such as participant or fly on the wall, direct or indirect through checklists and rating scales, and unstructured or focused on particular behaviours and practices. Participant observation is a powerful tool for the practitioner in examining the climate, relationships, behaviours, practices and activities taking place in the classroom. As a participant observer, the practitioner is actively involved in what is happening in the class-room, while having enough space to be able to function as a researcher. As this is an examination of classroom processes, the classroom teacher is in an ideal situation to collect data with the least interference in the natural processes occurring in the classroom. He or she is able to get first-hand experience and to record behaviour as it is taking place. A reflective diary/journal structured around the questions listed above, with a daily account of observations and reflections, is a very useful tool in the process of analysis (see Cooper 2006). The diary may also include notes on feedback from colleagues, discussions with pupils, parents and colleagues, and any other relevant information on the classroom.

Talking and reflecting with pupils, peers and parents

An important strategy in assessing the classroom situation is for the teacher to ask for the views of the pupils, colleagues and parents about the various aspects of the classroom. This feedback is not only useful in ensuring a more balanced assessment of the classroom situation, but it also enables the teacher to engage with the other stakeholders involved in a collaborative process of self-improvement. The questions listed above will help to direct the nature of the consultations with pupils, peers and parents. These may be in the form of:

- *individual or group semi-structured interviews*: face-to-face consultation not only ensures higher response rates but also makes it more likely to recruit the support and active collaboration of the participants concerned.

- *classroom reflections*: besides individual observation and reflection, the teacher may also engage in structured reflection with peers and the pupils themselves. The use of Circle Time is an excellent medium for engaging pupils in this discussion and reflection (for ways on how to organise Circle Time in the classroom see Chapter 4). These reflections can be noted in a classroom-reflective journal which may be separate from the teacher's own individual reflective diary.

- *peer observation*: data collected by a colleague about one's own practice is another useful strategy which helps the practitioner to get a different perspective on his or her own behaviour. The Classroom Systems Observation Scale (Fish and Dane 2000) is a helpful tool for structured classroom observations by peers.

Use of questionnaires and checklists

Checklists, questionnaires and rating scales may be used to examine either the whole classroom climate or parts of it, such as relationships, behaviour, engagement and sense of belonging. These should supplement rather than replace the more natural and direct participant observation and talking to pupils, colleagues and parents, and should be used sparingly. Observation and interviews remain the cornerstone of this assessment. Another issue with the use of most of the existing checklists is that they are based on individual pupils, rather than on the classroom as the unit of analysis. It may be still worthwhile, however, to have a look at some of the instruments available and their potential usefulness in the assessment. The practitioner may also develop his or her own checklist according to the needs of the classroom. Table 9.1 provides a list of some of the questionnaires and checklists which are available to the classroom practitioner.

STAGE 2   PLANNING FOR ACTION: WHERE DO WE WANT TO GO?

Once the data collected are analysed, the classroom practitioner may then draw a draft action plan for each assessed area (see Figure 9.2). The draft is discussed with the pupils, other colleagues and parents where relevant. The plan will seek to answer the following questions on each area of classroom functioning assessed as described in the previous section:

- What are the current strengths which need to be celebrated and maintained?

- What are the current weaknesses which we need to work on?

- What are the targets for improvement in this area? What specific changes do we need to make?

- What can help us to make these changes?

- What can hinder us from making these changes?

- What structures are already available which will facilitate these changes?

- Who is going to be involved in bringing about these changes? What exactly are we going to do as classroom practitioners and pupils (and others as appropriate) to bring about these changes?

- When are these changes going to take place?

- How long will it take to achieve the target?

- How will we know that the target has been achieved?

Table 9.1: List of checklists and questionnaires for the classroom practitioner

Name and author	Brief description
Create a Caring Classroom (Bluestein 2000)	An easy-to-use, informative checklist for the teacher to examine the socio-emotional climate in the classroom and the extent to which it addresses pupils' basic psychological needs. It is divided into four sections: the need for success; the need for belonging, dignity and respect; the need for power, structure and positivity; and the need for recognition, attention and emotional safety. The checklist may be downloaded at http://content.scholastic.com/browse/article.jsp?id=4428. A longer version of the checklist but focused on the school as a whole may be accessed at www.janebluestein.com/handouts/survey.html.
My Class Inventory (Short Form) (Fraser, Anderson and Wahlberg 1982)	Measures pupils' and teachers' actual and preferred views of the primary classroom environment. The scale consists of 25 items tapping five dimensions of the classroom environment: cohesiveness, friction, difficulty, satisfaction and competition. Pupils' discrepancy on the actual–preferred scores may serve as a basis of classroom intervention.
A Classroom Relationships Framework (Cefai 2004)	Seven items on educational engagement and socio-emotional competence are completed on all pupils by the classroom teacher; the global score gives an indication of peer relationships, problem solving and autonomy, and educational engagement. The individual scores are then aggregated to give a classroom score (see Figure 9.5 at the end of this chapter).
Assessing School Resilience Building (Henderson and Milstein 1996)	A teacher-completed scale measuring six aspects of resilience-building schools: prosocial bonding; clear, consistent boundaries; teaching life-skills; caring and support; high expectations; and opportunities for meaningful participation. An overall total score is computed. This scale, however, is focused on pupils, staff and the school rather than on classrooms.
SALAD (Olsen and Cooper 2001)	A systemic framework that helps the classroom practitioner analyse problem situations by identifying the patterns of interaction that create difficulties and the ways in which these may be altered. May be used to analyse the classroom relationships, including relationships with parents. The framework has five key areas, namely **S**ystems, **A**ccess, **L**imits, **A**cceptance and **D**irection.

Diagnosing Classroom Difficulty (Watkins and Wagner 2000)	A teacher framework to examine the various aspects of the psychosocial classroom climate in seeking to determine the nature of pupils' learning and behaviour difficulties.
Student–Teacher Relationship Scale (Pianta 2001)	A 28-item teacher-completed scale measuring three aspects of teacher–student relationships: conflict; closeness and affection; and over-dependence on the teacher.
Caring Teachers Framework (adapted from Sergiovanni 1994)	A checklist to assess the classroom teacher's relationships with his or her pupils (see Chapter 4).
Pupils' Perception of Teacher Checklist (Cefai 2008)	A checklist to examine pupils' views of their teacher and their relationship with him or her (see Chapter 4).
Sociometrics	An excellent tool to examine classroom relationships and create more harmonious relationships among the pupils (see Chapter 5).
Social Inclusion Survey (Fredrickson 1994)	A sociometric questionnaire on social acceptance by the peer group for children seven years and over.
ClassMaps Surveys (Doll, Zucker and Brehm 2004)	A sociometric strategy to assess classrooms as a whole. Pupils are asked to rate their classroom according to six characteristics of resilient classrooms: academic efficacy, academic self-determination, behavioural self-control, teacher–student relationships, peer relationships and home–school relationships. Individual pupil scores are then aggregated to provide a total score for the classroom.
Framework for Assessing Pupil Behaviour in the Classroom (developed from Cefai 2004)	Another easy-to-use checklist to assess peer relationships in the classroom (see Chapter 5).

continued on next page

Table 9.1: List of checklists and questionnaires for the classroom practitioner *continued*

Name and author	Brief description
The Strengths and Difficulties Questionnaire (Goodman 1997)	A teacher-friendly scale for identifying potential emotional, behavioural and social difficulties and strengths in the classroom (individually based). Includes parent and student (secondary) versions. It may be downloaded in various languages from www.sdqinfo.com.
Index for Inclusion (Booth and Ainscow 2002)	The index contains a list of indicators of inclusive cultures, policies and practices at the school, and is aimed to be used by the school staff in examining to what extent the school and classrooms are operating as inclusive communities.
Framework for Assessing Pupils' Orientation to Learning (Watkins 2003)	A framework to examine pupils' views on their engagement and learning in the classroom; it consists of a 12-item self-completed checklist (see Chapter 6).
Inventory About Learning Approaches (Cameron 1999)	Two self-administered questionnaires for 8–11-year-olds, one on 'What I do to learn' and the other on 'What stops my learning'. The questionnaires are intended to help the classroom teacher find what pupils perceive as positive and preventive factors in their learning and to plan individual approaches to classroom learning.
Framework for Enquiry into Pupils 'Feeling in Charge of Learning' (Watkins 2003)	A simple-to-use 11-item pupil-completed checklist into pupils' sense of autonomy in learning (see Chapter 8).
Rating Student Self-Regulated Learning Outcomes: A Teachers' Scale (Zimmerman and Martinez-Pons 1990)	An individually based, teacher-completed, 12-item rating scale focusing on pupils' use of self-regulation strategies in learning, such as seeking information, self-evaluation, goal setting and planning, seeking assistance and organisational activities.
Attitudes towards Home–School Collaboration (Eggertsdottir *et al.* 2005)	A teacher-completed, 16-item scale on the relationship and communication between the classroom teacher and parents (see Chapter 7).

Action plan

Strengths: things we are doing well in this area:

Weaknesses: things which we may do better in this area:

Targets for change in clear, specific language:

How can this change be brought about? What practices and behaviours need to take place?

What physical and human resources are already available both within and outside the classroom, which we can make use of in achieving the target?

What barriers may prevent us from reaching this target and how can they be removed?

Who will be involved in bringing about this change? How is their cooperation and engagement to be recruited?

When is this change going to take place? How long will it take to achieve the target? How would we know that the target has been achieved?

N.B. This form is to be filled for each area of the classroom context

Figure 9.2: An action plan for the classroom

In drawing up the action plan, it is very important to give added value to ideas coming from the pupils themselves. These are then discussed in terms of their practicality and manageability in the classroom. The use of Circle Time is a good vehicle for engaging the pupils in this activity. A copy of the plan may be sent to all parents via the pupils for their feedback and suggestions. Once the plan is finalised, it is then put into effect as agreed. It is essential not to be overambitious in bringing about change. One possibility is to work on one target from each area at one period of time (e.g. one target each in relationships, engagement, collaboration and inclusion); these may then be revised or replaced by other targets in the same area following evaluation.

STAGES 3 AND 4   ACTION AND REFLECTION: HOW ARE WE DOING? HOW FAR HAVE WE GONE?

Once the plan has been agreed upon by all members and a pupil-friendly version given to each pupil and made visible in a prominent place in the classroom, it is then implemented in the period of time set for intervention. Record keeping ensures commitment and motivation on all parts, and a monitoring chart displayed in the classroom is ticked regularly by both the classroom teacher and pupils at set times during the week. The chart monitors the progress made in each target for intervention in the view of both pupils and teacher. A scoring key may be agreed upon beforehand ranging from excellent progress to no progress at all, with agreed-upon criteria for success (see Figure 9.3). This phase of observation involves also the classroom practitioner going back to his or her reflective diary to write their reflections on the changes taking place. The reflections will serve for further planning and action. Once the period set for intervention is over, the teacher calls a Circle Time and, on the basis of the monitoring sheets and his or her reflective diaries and any other form of evaluation used, reviews the progress made and plans the next step for intervention in the area. A new action plan is drawn and set in motion collaboratively. Indeed this is a cyclical, ongoing model, and once the evaluation is finished, the process starts all over again.

ENDNOTE

Bringing about change in the classroom is not just about drawing up an action plan. Change requires vision, skills, incentives, resources *and* an action plan. When any of these are missing, the change is unlikely to be effective. Thousand and Villa's (1995) model of effective change (Figure 9.4) underlines the consequences and difficulties in effecting change when any of these elements are missing in our plan. Lack of vision will lead to confusion about where we want to go and where we will arrive eventually, while lack of incentives will result in

Target	Mon	Mon	Tue	Tue	Wed	Wed	Thu	Thu	Fri	Fri	*Tot Tr*	*Tot Pup*	*Tot*
Target 1 (R)													
Target 2 (P)													
Target 3 (I)													
Target 4 (C)													

Examples of targets
Target 1 (Relationships): We listen carefully when one of us is speaking
Target 2 (Participation): We have at least one game per day during lessons
Target 3 (Inclusion): We help each other during class work
Target 4 (Collaboration): We have at least one session of group work per day

Scores:
10–0 from excellent to no progress in this target

Agreed criteria for reaching target:
To be decided with the pupils

Agreed strategies to celebrate success:
To be decided with the pupils

Figure 9.3: A target behaviour monitoring chart

Vision	Skills	Incentives	Resources	Action plan	
Vision	Skills	Incentives	Resources	Action plan	CHANGE
	Skills	Incentives	Resources	Action plan	CONFUSION
Vision		Incentives	Resources	Action plan	ANXIETY
Vision	Skills		Resources	Action plan	RESISTANCE
Vision	Skills	Incentives		Action plan	FRUSTRATION
Vision	Skills	Incentives	Resources		TREADMILL

Figure 9.4: Managing effective change in the classroom (Thousand and Villa 1995)

resentment leading only to gradual change or none at all. Lack of the requisite knowledge and skills is set to raise the practitioner's anxiety level, while not having the necessary resources is likely to lead to frustration. Finally, we need a good plan of action, otherwise we will become embroiled in a process of false starts and a consequent waste of precious time and resources. It is essential for the classroom practitioner to ensure that all these qualities are on board before setting sail.

This voyage began with a positive and proactive vision of classrooms as resilience-enhancing communities for all pupils. It provided guidance and direction along the way, seeking to recruit your motivation to engage on the trip through setting out various success stories and accounts of colleagues already in action. It then presented the knowledge, tools and resources for you to set sail on your own.

It is hoped that, after having read this book, you will feel inspired and empowered to embark on your own voyage, taking concrete action to turn your classroom into a resilience-enhancing community. It is hoped that it will also be a pleasurable voyage.

Points for reflection

1. How does the framework presented in this chapter relate to your current classroom context? To what extent does it address the needs of your classroom in relation to the educational engagement and socio-emotional competence of your pupils?

2. How competent and confident do you feel in implementing this framework in your own classroom? What may help to increase your confidence and competence?

3. How practical and manageable do you think it is to implement the suggested plan of action in your classroom? What resources are already in place which might help you with the action research process? What barriers might prevent you from engaging in this venture? What and who might help you to overcome such obstacles? When do you think would be a reasonable date to start?

Classroom Relationships Framework

Complete for each pupil in your class, assigning 4 to 1 according to the frequency of the behaviour in class. Give your answers on the basis of the pupils' behaviour in class over the past months. Complete all items for each pupil as best as you can even if you are not absolutely certain.

4 = true for most of the time 3 = frequently true 2 = occasionally true 1 = rarely true	Gets along well with the other pupils	Likes to help the other pupils (with classwork, when upset or hurt, etc.)	Shares readily with the other pupils in class	Good at working through everyday classroom situations and difficulties	Able to think for him/herself	Seems interested to learn	Participates actively in the life of the class
Name/Index Number of Pupil							
1							
2							
3							
4							
5							
6							
7							
8							
9							
10							
11							
12							
13							
14							

Figure 9.5: A classroom relationships framework (Cefai 2004)

Name/Index Number of Pupil							
15							
16							
17							
18							
19							
20							
21							
22							
23							
24							
25							

Scoring and interpretation:

Add the columns for each pupil to get a total score for each of the seven items. The scores may be interpreted per column (item) or grouped in three clusters as follows:

- The first three items (1–3) are related to collaborative peer relationships and prosocial behaviour in the classroom.

- The next two items (4–5) tap problem solving and autonomy.

- The last two items (6–7) assess educational engagement in the classroom.

The averages may be worked out as frequency charts to have a visual representation of the level of the behaviour/cluster of behaviour in the class as a whole.

What pattern emerges about the pupils' socio-emotional competence and engagement in the classroom? What strengths could be celebrated and maintained? What aspects need to be improved? What changes do you need to make to bring about such an improvement?

Figure 9.5: A classroom relationships framework (Cefai 2004) *continued*

SUMMARY

- Effective classroom change needs to be introduced from within rather than from above, with the onus of responsibility being on the classroom practitioner together with the pupils, parents and colleagues. Any change has to be introduced in a way that fits in within the existing culture and needs of the classroom.

- Action research considers classroom practitioners, together with the pupils, parents and colleagues, to be those best placed to understand and analyse the classroom situation and introduce, implement and evaluate new practices accordingly.

- The first stage in the process of creating resilience-enhancing classrooms involves the analysis of the classroom situation in order to define the goals of intervention and prepare a plan of action. A set of questions about various aspects of classroom functioning is presented as a guide together with various methods of data collection. Natural and formative strategies such as participant observation and talking with pupils, colleagues and parents are the preferred modes of assessment, but information from checklists and questionnaires may also help to provide important information.

- The next stage is to draw up an action plan with clear and specific targets in the each of the areas selected; a template of such a plan is provided. The plan is then implemented in the classroom and monitored systematically. Finally, critical reflection and evaluation of the action plan are carried out with a view to further action to continue improving practice. This will ensure an ongoing process of action and reflection.

FURTHER READING

Baumfield, V., Hall, E. and Wall, K. (2008) *Action Research in the Classroom.* London: Sage Publications.

Brown, H. (2004) 'Action research in the classroom: a process that feeds the spirit of the adolescent.' *International Journal of Qualitative Methods 3*, 1 Article 3. Available at www.ualberta.ca/~iiqm/backissues/3_1/pdf/brown.pdf (accessed 12 December 2007).

Doveston, M. (2007) 'Developing capacity for social and emotional growth: an action research project.' *Pastoral Care in Education 25*, 2, 46–54.

Holly, M.L., Arhar, J. and Kasten, W. (2004) *Action Research for Teachers: Travelling the Yellow Brick Road,* 2nd edn. Upper Saddle River, NJ: Prentice-Hall.

Hopkins, D. (2002) *A Teacher's Guide to Classroom Research,* 3rd edn. Buckingham: Open University Press.

Meyers, E. and O'Connell Rust, F. (eds) (2003) *Taking Action with Teacher Research.* Portsmouth, NH: Heinemann.

Rust, F. and Clark, C. (2004) *How to do Action Research in Your Classroom: Lessons from the Teachers Network Leadership Institute.* Available at www.teachersnetwork.org/tnli/Action_Research_Booklet.pdf (accessed 22 November 2007).

UCERC Collaborative Partners (1999) *Teacher Research-Action Research Resources.* Available at: http://ucerc.edu/teacherresearch/teacherresearch.html (accessed 12 December 2007).

A Naturalistic Study of Classrooms

The study on which this book is based sought to examine the processes taking place in a number of primary school classrooms in Malta characterised by optimal learning environments. It aimed at capturing the common contextual processes that 'work' in classes consisting of both at-risk (low socio-economic status) and non-at-risk pupils. All the classes consisted of pupils coming from diverse socio-economic backgrounds. The focus of the study was on the classrooms themselves rather than individual children. Nine classrooms in three different primary schools from various regions in Malta were selected on the basis of a purposely constructed framework. This framework consisted of a questionnaire completed by classroom teachers, tapping into three components of educational resilience as defined in the study, namely:

- pupil prosocial behaviour in the classroom
- autonomy and problem solving
- motivation and engagement in classroom activities.

About six to eight weeks from the start of the scholastic year, all Year 2–4 teachers at the three schools were asked to complete the framework for each pupil in their classroom. By the end of the first scholastic term 22 out of 28 teachers had returned the completed instruments. The three classrooms in each school which appeared to have the highest levels of perceived prosocial behaviour, autonomy and problem solving, and educational engagement were selected for further study. The classes chosen ranged from Year 2 to Year 4 (6–9 years), with an average size of 20 boys and girls; all teachers were female. All classes were of mixed ability, and pupils came from diverse socio-economic backgrounds, although the exact nature of pupil intake varied from one classroom to the other. Year 1 classes were not included, since pupils in those classes would have just started attending the school. Year 5 and 6 pupils were also left out to avoid potential contamination of the processes being examined due to streaming on the basis of ability in those classes. At a later stage in the process two other teachers were asked to participate in the study to provide more data on some of the developing processes.

The study was an attempt to find out 'what actually goes on' in classes within a particular context through the exploration of the nature of the social phenomena. In seeking to understand these phenomena, it was crucial to study the meaning of the

experience and behaviour in context and in its full complexity, staying close to the
actors themselves and making full use of methods providing detail, depth and density
(cf. Guba and Lincoln 1981). Extended participant observation and semi-structured
interviews with the classroom teachers and pupils were the data collection methods
used. All teachers and pupils were relatively unknown to the researcher who thus
started the classroom observations as an outsider. Participant observation was spread
across the last five and a half months of the scholastic year, with one day per week in
each school. The researcher's role was that of 'observer as participant', focused on
observations with limited participation. This avoided the problems usually associated
with extended fieldwork, such as limiting the space needed to examine processes
without losing perspective of the group or context being studied, while still making
it possible to engage in a process of discovery with the participants. The researcher
took a more observant role during teacher explanations and a more active role during
class work, helping pupils in their work. Observation notes were written in a
fieldwork journal, which included a description of the activities observed, and
reflective comments on those observations. Observation guidelines were developed
from the literature and served as a loose framework for the observation of the
practices, behaviours, relationships and beliefs taking place in the classroom,
particularly in the initial stages of data collection. These included among other things
the nature of the communication and relationships between teachers and pupils and
among the pupils themselves, the participation of pupils in the classroom activities,
the expectations, beliefs and values of the classroom members, the classroom
management practices and pedagogical strategies.

During the last phase of the study individual semi-structured interviews were
held with the classroom teachers while focus groups were conducted with a small
number of pupils from each class. The interview schedules were developed from the
literature and, in line with the modified grounded theory analysis of the study, from
the themes that had emerged from the observations. The questions explored the
participants' views on the practices, activities, behaviours, relationships and beliefs
taking place in the classroom. The pupil interview guide explored their thoughts and
feelings about the classroom atmosphere, relationships, work, autonomy and
influence. The teachers' interview guide explored their perceptions of pupils'
behaviours, relationships and engagement as well as their views on the relationships,
collegiality and collaboration among staff, staff involvement in planning and
decision-making, and shared goals.

Analysis of the data commenced early on in the data-collection phase, with
interweaved data collection and analysis, both processes influencing one another. A
three-stage process characterised the analysis: an initial attempt to develop categories
which illuminated the data; 'saturating' these categories with many appropriate cases
in order to demonstrate their relevance; and finally developing these categories into a
more general analytical framework with relevance to the outside world (Glaser and
Strauss 1967). The emerging categories were drawn simultaneously from the
different classes, and were constantly compared to other examples from the data until

the researcher felt confident about their meaning and importance. The observation
and interview guidelines helped to keep the data collection focused on particular
aspects of the contexts being observed, but without seeking to verify or simply fit the
data within an existing framework. Such a perspective offered the possibility of
changing focus as the ongoing analysis of the rich data suggested. Mason's (1996)
dialectic perspective, combining an emphasis on prior theoretical ideas and models
that feed into and guide research, while at the same time seeking to generate theory
from the ongoing data analysis, guided the analysis of the data. Theory generation
was thus the result of the dual input of extant theory or 'orienting concepts' (Layder
1998) and emergent concepts. Orienting concepts helped to keep the data collection
focused on particular aspects of the classroom contexts, but they also affered the
possiblity of changing focus as the ongoing analysis of the rich data suggested. They
served as a good 'point of departure' to look at the data, to collect information, and to
think analytically about the data, and thence to develop theory.

References

Altenbaugh, R.J., Engel, D.E. and Martin, D.T. (1995) *Caring for Kids: A Critical Study of Urban School Leavers*. Bristol, PA: Falmer.

Anderman, E.A. (2002) 'School effects on psychological outcomes during adolescence.' *Journal of Educational Psychology 94*, 4, 795–809.

Anthony, E.J. (1974) 'The Syndrome of the Psychologically Invulnerable Child.' In E.J. Anthony and C. Koupernick (eds) *The Child in His Family: Children at Psychiatric Risk*. New York: Wiley.

Bandura, A. (1993) 'Perceived self efficacy in cognitive development and functioning.' *Educational Psychologist 28*, 2, 117–148.

Bandura, A. (1997) *Self Efficacy: The Exercise of Control*. New York: Freeman.

Bartolo, P., Janik, I., Janikova,V., Hofsass, T. *et al.* (2007) *Responding to Student Diversity: Teacher's Handbook*. Malta: University of Malta.

Battistisch, V. (2001) 'Effects of an Elementary School Intervention on Students' "Connectedness" to School and Social Adjustment During Middle School.' *Resilience in Education: Theoretical, Interactive and Empirical Applications*. Symposium conducted at the annual meeting of the American Educational Research Association, Seattle, WA.

Battistisch, V., Solomon, D. and Delucchi, K. (1993) 'Interaction processes and student outcomes in cooperative learning groups.' *Elementary School Journal 94*, 1, 19–32.

Battistisch, V., Solomon, D., Dong-il, K., Watson, M. and Schaps, E. (1995) 'Schools as communities, poverty levels of student populations, and students' attitudes, motives and performance: a multilevel analysis.' *American Educational Research Journal 32*, 627–658.

Battistisch, V., Solomon, D., Watson, M. and Schaps, E. (1997) 'Caring school communities.' *Educational Psychologist 32*, 3, 137–151.

Benard, B. (1991) *Fostering Resiliency in Kids: Protective Factors in the Family, School and Community*. San Francisco: Far West Laboratory for Educational Research and Development.

Bluestein, J. (2000) 'Create a caring classroom.' *Instructor 110*, 2, 35–37. Available at http://content.scholastic.com/browse/article.jsp?id=4428 (accessed 22 November 2007).

Booth, T. and Ainscow, M. (2002) *Index for Inclusion: Developing Learning and Participation in School*, rev. edn. Bristol: CSIE.

Bronfenbrenner, U. (1979) *The Ecology of Human Development*. Cambridge, MA: Harvard University Press.

Bronfenbrenner, U. (1989) 'Ecological systems theory.' *Annals of Child Development 6*, 187–249.

Brown, J.H. (2004) 'Emerging Social Constructions in Educational Policy, Research and Practice.' In H.C. Waxman, Y.N. Padron and J.P. Gray (eds) *Educational Resiliency: Student, Teacher, and School Perspectives*. Greenwich, CT: Information Age Publishing.

Brown, J.H., D'Emidio-Caston, M. and Benard, B. (2001) *Resilience Education*. Thousand Oaks, CA: Corwin Press.

Brown, S., Riddell, S. and Duffield, J. (1996) 'Responding to Pressures: A Study of Four Secondary Schools.' In P. Wood (ed.) *Contemporary Issues in Teaching and Learning*. London: Routledge.

Bryk, A.S. and Driscoll, M.E. (1988) *The School as Community: Theoretical Foundations, Contextual Influences, and Consequences for Students and Teachers*. Madison, WI: National Center on Effective Secondary Schools, University of Wisconsin.

Bryk, A., Camburn, E. and Louis, K.L. (1999) 'Professional community in Chicago Elementary School: facilitating factors and organizational consequences.' *Educational Administration Quarterly 35*, Supplement, 751–781. Available at www.eric.ed.gov/ERICDocs/data/ericdocs2sql/content_storage_01/0000 019b/80/15/02/76.pdf (accessed 22 November 2007).

Calderwood, P. (2000) *Learning Community: Finding Common Ground in Difference*. New York: Teachers College Press.

Cameron, S. (1999) 'Inventory About Learning Approaches.' In S. Cameron (ed.) *Self-Regulated Learning and Behaviour.* London: NFER-NELSON.

Cappella, E. and Weinstein, R.S. (2001) 'Turning around reading achievement: predictors of high school students' academic resilience.' *Journal of Educational Psychology, 93,* 758–771.

Caprara, G.V., Pastorelli, C., Bandura, A. and Zimbardo, P.G. (2000) 'Prosocial foundations of children's academic achievement.' *Psychological Science 53,* 2, 302–306.

Carter, K. and Doyle, W. (2006) 'Classroom Management in Early Childhood and Elementary Classrooms.' In C. Everston and C. Weinstein (eds) *Handbook of Classroom Management: Research Practice and Contemporary Issues.* London: Lawrence Erlbaum Associates.

Catalano, R.F. and Hawkins, J.D. (1996) 'The Social Developmental Model: A Theory of Antisocial Behaviour.' In J.D. Hawkins (ed.) *Delinquency and Crime: Current Theories.* New York: Cambridge University Press.

Catterall, J.S. (1998) 'Risk and resilience in student transitions to high school.' *American Journal of Education 106,* 302–333.

Cefai, C. (2004) 'Pupil resilience in the classroom: a teachers' framework.' *Emotional and Behavioural Difficulties 9,* 3, 149–170.

Cefai, C. (2007) 'Resilience for all: a study of classrooms as protective contexts.' *Emotional and Behavioural Difficulties 12,* 2, 119–134.

Chirkov, V. and Ryan, R.M. (2001) 'Parent and teacher autonomy-support in Russian and US adolescents: common effects on well-being and academic motivation.' *Journal of Cross Cultural Psychology 32,* 618–635.

Condly, S.J. (2006) 'Resilience in children: a review of literature with implications for education.' *Urban Education 41,* 3, 211–236.

Connell, J.P. and Wellborn, J.G. (1991) 'Competence, Autonomy and Relatedness: A Motivational Analysis of Self-system Processes.' In M.R.S. Gunnar (ed.) *Self Processes and Development.* Hillsdale, NJ: Lawrence Erlbaum Associates.

Connell, J.P., Halpern-Felsher, B.L., Clifford, E., Crichslow, W. and Usinger, P. (1995) 'Hanging in there: behavioural, psychological and contextual factors affecting whether African American adolescents stay in high school.' *Journal of Adolescent Research 10,* 1, 41–63.

Cook-Sather, E. (2002) 'Authorizing students' perspectives: towards trust, dialogue and change in education.' *Educational Researcher 31,* 4, 3–14.

Cooper, P. (2006) *Promoting Positive Pupil Engagement: Educating Pupils with Social, Emotional and Behaviour Difficulties.* Malta: Miller Publications.

Cooper, P., Drummond, M., Hart, S., Lovey, J. and McLaughlin, C. (2000) *Positive Alternatives to Exclusion.* London: Routledge.

Criss, M.M., Pettit, G.S., Bates, J.E., Dodge, K.A. and Lapp, A.L. (2002) 'Family adversity, positive peer relationships, and children's externalising behaviour: a longitudinal perspective on risk and resilience.' *Child Development 73,* 4, 1220–1237.

Crone, L.J. and Teddlie, C. (1995) 'Further examination of teacher behaviour in differentially effective schools: selection and socialization processes.' *Journal of Classroom Interaction 30,* 1, 1–9.

Crosnoe, R. and Elder, G. (2004) 'Family dynamics, supportive relationships, and educational resilience during adolescence.' *Journal of Family Issues 25,* 5, 571–602.

Daniels, H., Cole, T. and Reykebill, N. (1999) *Emotional and Behaviour Difficulties in Mainstream Schools.* London: DfEE.

Dasho, S., Lewis, C. and Watson, M. (2001) 'Fostering Emotional Intelligence in the Classroom and School: Strategies from the Child Development Project.' In J. Cohen (ed.) *Caring Classrooms/Intelligent Schools: The Social Emotional Education of Young Children.* New York: Teachers College Press.

Davies, H.A. (2003) 'Conceptualizing the role and influence of student–teacher relationships on children's social and cognitive development.' *Educational Psychologist 38,* 4, 207–234.

Deci, E.L. and Ryan, R.M. (1985) *Intrinsic Motivation and Self-determination in Human Behaviour.* New York: Plenum.

Deci, E.L. and Ryan, R.M. (1995) 'Human Autonomy: The Basis for True Self-esteem.' In M. Kermis (ed.) *Efficacy, Agency and Self-esteem.* New York: Plenum.

Deci, E.L., Vallerand, R.J., Pelleiter, L.G. and Ryan, R.M. (1991) 'Motivation and education: the self determination perspective.' *Educational Psychologist 26,* 325–346.

Dent, R. and Cameron, R.J. (2003) 'Developing resilience in children who are in public care: the educational psychology perspective.' *Educational Psychology in Practice 19,* 1, 3–19.

Department for Education and Employment (DfEE) (2004) *Excellence and Enjoyment: Social and Emotional Aspects of Learning.* London: HMSO.

DeRosier, M., Kupersmidt, J.B. and Patterson, C.J. (1994) 'Children's academic and behavioral adjustment as a function of the chronicity and proximity of peer rejection.' *Child Development 65*, 1799–1813.

Doll, B., Zucker, S. and Brehm, C. (2004) *Resilient Classrooms: Creating Healthy Environments for Learning.* New York: The Guilford Press.

Eggertsdottir, R., Marinosson, G.L., Sigales, C., Audunsdottir, I. *et al.* (2005) *Pathways to Inclusion: A Guide for Staff Development.* Reykjavik: University of Iceland Press.

Eisner, E. (1998) *The Enlightened Eye: Qualitative Inquiry and the Enhancement of Educational Practice.* Upper Saddle River, NJ: Merrill.

Elias, M.J. (2001) 'Prepare children for the tests of life, not a life of tests.' *Education Week 21*, 4, 40.

Elias, M.J. and Weissberg, R. (2000) 'Primary prevention: educational approaches to enhance social and emotional learning.' *Journal of School Health 70*, 5, 186–194.

Elias, M.J., Arnold, H. and Steiger Hussey, C. (2003) 'EQ, IQ, and Effective Learning and Leadership.' In M.J. Elias, H. Arnold and C. Steiger Hussey (eds) *EQ+IQ=Best Leadership Practices for Caring and Successful Schools.* Thousand Oaks, CA: Corwin Press.

Fish, M.C. and Dane, E. (2000) 'The Classroom Systems Observation Scale: development of an instrument to assess classrooms using a systems perspective.' *Learning Environments Research 3*, 67–92.

Fraser, B.J. (1994) 'Research on Classroom and School Climate.' In D.L. Gabel (ed.) *Handbook of Research on Science Teaching and Learning.* New York: Macmillan Publishing.

Fraser, B.J., Anderson, G.J. and Wahlberg, H.J. (1982) *Assessment of Learning Environments: Manual for Learning Environment Inventory (LEI and My Class Inventory).* Perth: Australian Institute of Technology.

Fredrickson, N. (1994) 'School Inclusion Survey (SIS).' In N. Fredrickson and B. Graham (eds) *Social Skills and Emotional Intelligence.* London: NFER-NELSON.

Freiberg, H.J., Stein, T.A. and Huang, S.L. (1995) 'The effects of classroom management intervention on student achievement in inner city elementary schools.' *Educational Research and Evaluation 1*, 1, 33–66.

Fullan, M. (1991) *The New Meaning of Educational Change.* New York: Teachers College Press.

Garmezy, N. (1971) 'Vulnerable research and the issue of primary prevention.' *Journal of Orthopsychiatry 41*, 101–116.

Garmezy, N. and Rutter, M. (1983) *Stress, Coping and Development in Children.* New York: McGraw-Hill.

Garmezy, N., Masten, A.S. and Tellegen, A. (1984) 'The study of stress and competence in children: a building block for developmental psychopathology.' *Child Development, 55*, 97–111.

Geake, J.G. (2006) 'The neurological basis of intelligence: a contrast with "brain-based" education.' *Education-Line.* Available at www.leeds.ac.uk/educol/documents/156074.htm (accessed 22 November 2007).

Geake, J.G. and Cooper, P.W. (2003) 'Implications of cognitive neuroscience for education.' *Westminster Studies in Education 26*, 10, 7–20.

Glaser, B.G. and Strauss, A.M. (1967) *The Discovery of Grounded Theory: Strategies for Qualitative Research.* New York: Aldine.

Glaser, W. (1990) *The Quality School: Managing Students without Coercion.* New York: Harper Perennial.

Goodenow, C. (1993) 'Classroom belonging among early adolescent students: relationships to motivation and achievement.' *Journal of Early Adolescence 13*, 21–43.

Goodman, R. (1997) 'The Strengths and difficulties questionnaire: A research note.' *Journal of Child Psychiatry and Psychology 38*, 8, 581–85.

Guba, E.G. and Lincoln, Y.S. (1981) *Effective Evaluation.* San Francisco, CA: Jossey-Bass.

Gurtner, J.L., Monnard, I. and Genoud, P.A. (2001) 'Towards a Multilayered Model of Context and Its Impact on Motivation.' In S. Volet and S. Jarvela (eds) *Motivation in Learning Contexts: Theoretical Advances and Methodological Implications.* London: Pergamon.

Hawkins, J.D., Catalano, R.F., Kosterman, R., Abbott, R. and Hill, K.G. (1999) 'Preventing adolescent health risk behaviours by strengthening protection during childhood.' *Archives of Pediatrics and Adolescent Medicine 153*, 226–234.

Henderson, N. and Milstein, M.M. (1996) *Resiliency in Schools: Making it Happen for Students and Educators.* Thousand Oaks, CA: Corwin Press.

Hopkins, D. (2002) *A Teacher's Guide to Classroom Research*, 3rd edn. Buckingham: Open University Press.

Houghton, P. (2001) 'Finding allies: sustaining teachers' health and well-being.' *Phi Delta Kappa 82*, 9, 706–712.

Huggins, P. (1997) *Creating a Caring Classroom.* Longmont, CO: Sopris West.

Johnson, D.W. and Johnson, R.T. (1991) 'Cooperative Learning and Classroom and School Learning.' In B.J. Fraser and H.J. Walberg (eds) *Educational Environments: Evaluations, Antecedents and Consequences.* London: Pergamon.

Johnson, D.W., Johnson, R.T. and Stanne, M.B. (2000) Cooperative Learning Methods: A Meta Analysis. Available at www.co-operation.org/pages/cl-methods.html (accessed 8 February 2008).

Kidder, R. (1990) 'Should schools pay the price of prison?' *Christian Science Monitor 13*, 127–132.

Kohn, A. (1996) *Beyond Discipline: From Compliance to Community.* Alexandra, VA: ASCD.

Krovetz, M.L. (1999) *Fostering Resiliency: Expecting All Students to Use Their Minds and Hearts as Well.* Thousand Oaks, CA: Corwin Press.

Kyriacu, C. (1996) 'Teacher stress: a review of some international comparisons.' *Education Section Review 20*, 1, 17–20.

Kyriakides, L., Campbell, R.J. and Gagatsis, A. (2000) 'The significance of the classroom effect in primary schools: an application of Creemers' comprehensive model of educational effectiveness.' *School Effectiveness and School Improvement 11*, 4, 501–529.

Layard, R. (2005) *Happiness: Lessons from a New Science.* London: Penguin.

Layder, D. (1998) *Sociological Practice: Linking Theory and Social Research.* London: Sage Publications.

Levine, D.A. (2003) *Building Classroom Communities.* Bloomington, IN: National Educational Service.

Lewis, C., Schaps, E. and Watson, M. (1999) 'Recapturing Education's Full Mission: Educating for Social, Ethical, and Intellectual Development.' In C. Reigeluth (ed.) *Instructional-Design Theories and Models: A New Paradigm of Instructional Theory.* Mahwah, NJ: Lawrence Erlbaum Associates.

Lewis, C., Watson, M. and Schaps, E. (2003) 'Building Community in School.' In M.J. Elias, H. Arnold and C. Steiger Hussey (eds) *EQ+IQ=Best Leadership Practices for Caring and Successful Schools.* Thousand Oaks, CA: Corwin Press.

Liddle, H.A. (1994) 'Contextualizing Resilience.' In M.C. Wang and E.W. Goron (eds) *Educational Resilience in Inner-City America: Challenges and Opportunities.* Hillsdale, NJ: Erlbaum.

Linnenbrink, E.A. and Pintrich, P.R. (2003) 'The role of self-efficacy in student engagement and learning in the classroom.' *Reading and Writing Quarterly: Overcoming Learning Difficulties 19*, 2, 119–137.

Lubeck, S. and Garrett, P. (1990) 'The social construction of the "at risk" child.' *British Journal of Sociology of Education 11*, 3, 327–340.

Luthar, S.S., Cicchetti, D. and Becker, B. (2000) 'The construct of resilience: a critical evaluation and guidelines for future work.' *Child Development 71*, 3, 543–562.

Lynch, M. and Cicchetti, D. (1992) 'Maltreated Children's Reports of Relatedness to Their Teachers.' In R.C. Pianta (ed.) *Beyond the Parent: The Role of Other Adults in Children's Lives.* San Francisco, CA: Jossey-Bass.

Manke, M.P. (1997) *Classroom Power Relations: Understanding Student–Teacher Interaction.* Mahwah, NJ: Lawrence Erlbaum Associates.

Maslow, A. (1970) *Motivation and Personality.* New York: Harper & Row.

Mason, J. (1996) *Qualitative Researching.* London: Sage.

Masten, A.S. and Coatsworth, J.D. (1998) 'The development of competence in unfavourable environments: lessons from research on successful children.' *American Psychologist 53*, 2, 205–220.

McLaughlin, M.W. (1993) 'What Matters Most in Teachers' Workplace Context?' In J.W.M. Little (ed.) *Teachers' Work: Individuals, Colleagues, and Contexts.* New York: Teachers College Press.

McLaughlin, M.W. and Talbert, J. (2006) *Building School-Based Teacher Learning Communities.* New York: Teachers College Press.

Moos, R. (1991) 'Connections between School, Work and Family Settings.' In B. Fraser and H. Walberg (eds) *Educational Environments.* Oxford: Pergamon.

Mosley, J. (1993) *Turn Your School Round.* Wisbech, Cambridgeshire: LDA.

Mosley, J. and Tew, M. (1999) *Quality Circle Time in the Secondary School – A Handbook of Good Practice.* London: David Fulton Publishers.

Muijs, D. and Reynolds, D. (2001) *Effective Teaching: Evidence and Practice.* London: Paul Chapman.

Newman, B.M., Myers, M.C., Newman, P.R., Lohman, B.J. and Smith, V.L. (2000) 'The transition to high school for academically promising, urban, low-income African American youth.' *Adolescence 35*, 137, 45–66.

Newman, F.M., Wehlage, G.G. and Lamborn, S.D. (1992) 'The Significance and Sources of Student Engagement.' In F.M. Newman (ed.) *Student Engagement and Achievement in American Secondary Schools.* New York: Teachers College Press.

Nias, J. (1999) 'Primary Teaching as a Culture of Care.' In J. Prosser (ed.) *School Culture.* London: Paul Chapman.

Nicholls, J.G. (1989) *The Competitive Ethos and Democratic Education.* Cambridge, MA: Harvard University Press.

Noddings, N. (1998) 'Schools face crisis in caring.' *Education Week 8*, 14, 32.

Noddings, N. (1992) *The Challenge to Schools.* New York: Teachers College Press.

Noddings, N. (1995) 'Teaching themes of care.' *Phi Delta Kappa 96*, 675–679.

Oldfather, P. (1993) 'What students say about motivating experiences in a whole language classroom.' *The Reading Teacher 46*, 672–678.

Olsen, J. and Cooper, P. (2001) *Dealing with Disruptive Students in the Classroom*. London: Kogan Page.

Organisation for Economic Co-operation and Development (OECD) (1995) *Our Children at Risk*. Paris: OECD.

Osterman, F.K. (2000) 'Students' need for belonging in the school community.' *Review of Educational Research 70*, 323–367.

Padron, Y.N., Waxman, H.C. and Huang, S.L. (1999) 'Classroom and instructional learning: environment differences between resilient and non-resilient elementary school students.' *Journal of Education for Students Placed at Risk 4*, 1, 63–81.

Parker, J.G. and Asher, S.R. (1997) 'Peer relations and later personal adjustment: are low-accepted children at risk?' *Psychological Bulletin 102*, 3, 357–389.

Pianta, R.C. (1997) 'Adult–child relationship process and early schooling.' *Early Education and Development 8*, 11–26.

Pianta, R.C. (1999) *Enhancing Relationships between Children and Teachers*. Washington, DC: American Psychological Association.

Pianta, R.C. (2001) *Student–Teacher Relationship Scale*. Washington, DC: American Psychological Association.

Pianta, R.C. and Sternberg, M. (1992) 'Teacher–Child Relationships and the Process of Adjusting to School.' In R.C. Pianta (ed.) *Beyond the Parent: The Role of Other Adults in Children's Lives*. San Francisco, CA: Jossey-Bass.

Pianta, R.C. and Walsh, D.J. (1998) 'Applying the construct of resilience in schools: cautions from a developmental systems perspective.' *School Psychology Review 27*, 3, 407–417.

Pomeroy, E. (2000) *Experiencing Exclusion*. Stoke on Trent: Trentham.

Poulou, M. (2007) 'Social resilience within a social and emotional learning framework: the perceptions of teachers in Greece.' *Emotional and Behavioural Difficulties 12*, 2, 91–104.

Rees, P. and Bailey, K. (2003) 'Positive exceptions: learning from students who "beat the odds."' *Educational and Child Psychology 20*, 4, 41–59.

Resnick, M.D., Bearman, P.S., Blum, R.W., Bauman, K.E., Harris, L.J. and Jones, J. (1997) 'Protecting adolescents from harm: findings from the national longitudinal study on adolescent health.' *Journal of the American Medical Association 278*, 823–832.

Rogers, C. (1998) 'Teacher Expectations: Implications for School Improvement.' In D. Shorrocks-Taylor (ed.) *Directions in Educational Psychology*. London: Whurr Publishers.

Rutter, M. (1990) 'Psychosocial Resilience and Protective Mechanisms.' In A. Rolf, D. Masten, K. Cicchetti, K. Neuchterlein and S. Weintraub (eds) *Risk and Protective Factors in the Development of Psychopathology*. New York: Cambridge University Press.

Rutter, M. (1991) 'Childhood experiences and adult psychosocial functioning.' *Ciba Foundation Symposium*, 189–200.

Rutter, M., Maughan, B., Mortimore, P. and Ouston, J. (1979) *Fifteen Thousand Hours: Secondary Schools and Their Effects on Children*. London: Open Books.

Ryan, R.M. (1995) 'Psychological needs and the facilitation of integrative processes.' *Journal of Personality 63*, 3, 397–427.

Ryan, R. and Powelson, C. (1991) 'Autonomy and relatedness as fundamental to motivation and education.' *Journal of Experimental Education 60*, 49–66.

Saskatchewan Education (1995) *Social Studies: A Curriculum Guide for the Elementary Level*. Available at www.sasked.gov.sk.ca/docs/elemsoc/g2u31ess.html (accessed 26 January 2008).

Schoon, I. (2006) *Risk and Resilience: Adaptations in Changing Times*. Cambridge: Cambridge University Press.

Semmens, R.A. (1999) *Full-Service Schooling: 'At Risk' Students and Democratic Citizenship*. Brighton: BERA Conference.

Sergiovanni, T.J. (1994) *Building School Communities*. San Francisco, CA: Jossey-Bass.

Sergiovanni, T.J. (1996) 'Learning community, professional community and the school as a centre of inquiry.' *Principal Matters*, April, 1–4.

Shann, M.H. (1999) 'Academics and a culture of caring.' *School Effectiveness and School Improvement 10*, 4, 390–413.

Slavin, R.E. (1991) *Student Team Learning: A Practical Guide to Cooperative Learning*, 3rd edn. Washington, DC: National Education Association.

Solomon, D., Watson, M., Battistisch, V., Schaps, E. and Delucchi, K. (1992) 'Creating a Caring Community: Educational Practices that Promote Children's Prosocial Development.' In F.K. Oser, A. Dick and J. Patry (eds) *Effective and Responsible Teaching: The New Synthesis*. San Francisco, CA: Jossey-Bass.

Solomon, D., Watson, M., Battistisch, V., Schaps, E. and Delucchi, K. (1997a) 'Creating classrooms that students experience as communities.' *American Journal of Community Psychology 24*, 6, 719–748.

Solomon, D., Battistisch, V., Il-Kim, D. and Watson, M. (1997b) 'Teacher practices associated with students' sense of the classroom as a community.' *Social Psychology of Education 1*, 235–267.

Solomon, D., Battistisch, V., Watson, M., Schaps, E. and Lewis, C. (2000) 'A six-district study of educational change: direct and mediated effects of the child development project.' *Social Psychology of Education 4*, 3–51.

Thousand, J.S. and Villa, R.A. (1995) 'Managing Complex Change Toward Inclusive Schooling.' In R.A. Villa and Thousand (eds) *Creating an Inclusive Classroom.* Alexandria, VA: Association for Supervision and Curriculum Development.

Tomlinson, C.A. (1999) *The Differentiated Classroom: Responding to the Needs of All Learners.* Alexandria, VA: ASCD.

Tomlinson, C.A. (2001) *How to Differentiate Instruction in Mixed Ability Classrooms.* Alexandria, VA: ASCD.

Topping, K.J., Bremner, W.G. and Holmes, E.A. (2000) 'Social Competence: The Social Construction of the Concept.' In R. Bar-On and J.D.A. Parker (eds) *The Handbook of Emotional Intelligence: Theory, Development, Assessment, and Application at Home, School, and in the Workplace.* San Fransisco, CA: Jossey-Bass.

Turner, J.C. and Meyer, D.K. (2000) 'Studying and understanding the instructional contexts of classrooms: using our past to forget our future.' *Educational Psychologist 35*, 69–85.

Wang, M.C. and Haertel, G.D. (1995) 'Educational Resilience.' In M.C. Wang, M.C. Reynolds and H.J. Walberg (eds) *Handbook of Special Education: Research and Practice.* New York: Pergamon.

Wang, M.C., Haertel, G.D. and Walberg, H.J. (1993) 'Synthesis of research: what helps students learn?' *Educational Leadership 51*, 4, 74–79.

Watkins, C. (2001) *Learning about Learning Enhances Performance.* London: Institute of Education School Improvement Network, Research Matters Series No. 13.

Watkins, C. (2003) *Learning: A Sense-maker Guide.* London: Association of Teachers and Lecturers.

Watkins, C. (2005) *Classrooms as Learning Communities. What's In It for Schools?* Oxford: Routledge.

Watkins, C. and Wagner, P. (2000) *Improving School Behaviour.* London: Sage/Paul Chapman.

Watkins, C., Carnell, E., Lodge, C., Wagner, P. and Whalley, C. (2002) *Effective Learning.* London: Institute of Education School Improvement Network.

Waxman, H.C., Brown, A. and Chang, H. (2004) 'Future Directions for Educational Resiliency Research.' In H.C. Waxman, Y.N. Padron and J.P. Gray (eds) *Educational Resiliency: Student, Teacher, and School Perspectives.* Greenwich, CT: Information Age Publishing.

Waxman, H.C., Huang, S.L. and Wang, M.C. (1997a) 'Motivation and learning environment differences between resilient and non-resilient Latino middle school students.' *Hispanic Journal of Behavioural Sciences 19*, 137–155.

Waxman, H.C., Huang, S.L. and Wang, M.C. (1997b) 'Investigating the multilevel classroom learning environment of resilient and non-resilient students from inner-city elementary schools.' *International Journal of Educational Research 27*, 343–353.

Weare, K. (2000) *Promoting Mental, Emotional + Social Health: A Whole School Approach.* London and New York: Routledge.

Wehlage, G.G., Rutter, R.A., Smith, G.A., Lesko, N. and Fernandez, R. (1989) *Reducing the Risk: Schools as Communities of Support.* London: Falmer Press.

Wentzel, K.R. (1997) 'Student motivation in middle school: the role of perceived pedagogical caring.' *Journal of Educational Psychology 89*, 3, 411–419.

Wentzel, K.R. (1998) 'Social relationships and motivation in middle school: the role of parents, teachers, and peers.' *Journal of Educational Psychology 90*, 2, 202–209.

Wentzel, K.R. and Asher, S.R. (1995) 'The academic lives of neglected, rejected, popular, and controversial children.' *Child Development 66*, 754–763.

Werner, E. (1990) 'Protective Factors and Individual Resilience.' In S.J.S. Meisels (ed.) *Handbook of Early Childhood Intervention.* Cambridge: Cambridge University Press.

Werner, E. and Smith, R. (1988) *Vulnerable but Invincible: A Longitudinal Study of Resilient Children and Youth.* New York: Adams, Bannister and Cox.

Werner, E. and Smith, R. (1992) *Overcoming the Odds: High-Risk Children from Birth to Adulthood.* New York: Cornell University Press.

Westheimer, J. (1998) *Among School Teachers.* New York: Teachers College Press.

Willms, J.D. (2003) *Student Engagement at School: A Sense of Belonging and Participation. Results from PISA 2000.* Paris: OECD.

Wilson, B. and Corbett, H.D. (2001) *Listening to Urban Kids: School Reform and the Teachers They Want.* Albany, NY: State University of New York Press.

Zimmerman, B.J. and Martinez-Pons, M. (1990) *Rating Student Self-Regulated Learning Outcomes: A Teacher's Scale (RSSRL).* Washington, DC: American Psychological Association.

Subject Index

Author Index

Waxman, H.C. 21, 25, 29,
    33, 84
Weare, K. 32
Wehlage, G.G. 26, 28
Weinstein, R.S. 21
Weissberg, R. 25
Wellborn, J.G. 34, 43, 56
Wentzel, K.R. 43, 56, 70,
    118
Werner, E. 22, 23, 32, 56
Westheimer, J. 33, 47
Willms, J.D. 56
Wilson, B. 122

Zimmerman, B.J. 150
Zucker, S. 149